# WOMEN DEACONS

## PAST, PRESENT, FUTURE

Gary Macy,
William T. Ditewig,
and
Phyllis Zagano

FOREWORD BY Susan A. Ross

Paulist Press
New York / Mahwah, NJ

Cover photograph by Rev. Gordon Plumb. Church of All Saints, St. Radegund, Cambridge, England.

Cover and book design by Lynn Else

Library of Congress Cataloging-in-Publication Data

Macy, Gary.
    Women deacons : past, present, future / Gary Macy, William T. Ditewig, and Phyllis Zagano.
        p. cm.
    Includes bibliographical references (p.      ).
    ISBN 978-0-8091-4743-4 (alk. paper) — ISBN 978-1-61643-052-8 1. Deaconesses—Catholic Church. I. Ditewig, William T. II. Zagano, Phyllis. III. Title.
    BX1912.2.M33 2012
    262'.14208209—dc23

                                                        2011028281

Published by Paulist Press
997 Macarthur Boulevard
Mahwah, New Jersey 07430

www.paulistpress.com

Printed and bound in the
United States of America

# CONTENTS

# FOREWORD

## Susan A. Ross

Since I began teaching over thirty years ago, I have given many lectures on women's issues to various audiences, many of them in parishes. In the last ten years, I have also traveled three times to Kenya and have had the privilege of learning from the many women active in ministry in Eastern Africa. In nearly every one of these lectures and discussions, the issue of women's ordained ministry inevitably arises. Women who are hospital chaplains ask why they cannot bless and anoint the patients at whose bedside they have ministered, but must wait for a priest, often someone unknown to the patient and family, to come and "officially" minister the sacrament. Women who work in parishes tell stories of being summarily fired by a new pastor since they have no official standing in the Church. And women who are gifted scholars and preachers are unable to break open the Word of God in the Eucharistic Liturgy, since only an ordained person can "legitimately" preach. Yet, women are the backbone of the Church, as we all know. Without the dedicated work of so many women, the Church would collapse.

Since 1976, the Roman Catholic Church has repeatedly stated that women cannot be ordained to the priesthood. But the question of women's ordination to the diaconate remains open. Since the permanent diaconate was restored at Vatican II, many men, not a few of them married, have gone through the process of study and formation for ordination to the diaconate; currently there are over 17,000 permanent deacons in the United States. The wives of these married deacons often go through the same formation and study with their husbands, and in my own experience of teaching these candidates, they are often more educated and qualified for diaconal work than many of the male candidates. Some are told that during this process they must be silent and cannot ask any questions; as with the admonition in 1 Timothy 2:12, they can only ask their husbands questions later at home! So women remain excluded from the ranks of the clergy. Some women, frustrated with the slow pace of progress for women's inclusion in the Church, have left Catholicism and have sought ordination in other denominations. Others have taken matters into their own hands and sought priestly ordination in the "Roman Catholic Womenpriests" movement. And every day, millions of women serve the Church through their ministries in education, charity, and liturgy but lack any official recognition of their gifts or participation in Church governance.

Gary Macy, William Ditewig, and Phyllis Zagano have thus performed an invaluable service in writing *Women Deacons: Past, Present, Future.* To the question of whether there is historical precedent for women being ordained to the diaconate, Gary Macy offers ample evidence for women's official *and* clerical ministry in the Church. He also shows how this practice was first discouraged and then ended. What "ordination" means has actually changed over time, Macy shows, and the distinctive developments in the late medieval Church that excluded women once and for all from ordained diaconal ministry are revealed for their misogyny. William Ditewig, himself an ordained deacon, examines the present state of the issue. He works through the documents of and following Vatican II, showing how the question of women's diaconal ministry has arisen over and over and why it is time for this issue to be resolved. Lastly, Phyllis Zagano, already an authority on the issue of women and the diaconate, looks toward the future, showing the benefits and possibilities that the ordination of women to the diaconate would bring to the Church.

This book could hardly be more timely. What a difference women's presence as official ministers of the Church would make to parish ministry: Imagine if women could witness marriages and baptisms as well as offer their wisdom and counsel to couples approaching these sacraments! Imagine if women's gifts of preaching were available to their congregations! Consider as well what difference it would make if women had had governing roles in dioceses and had status as clergy when questions of clerical conduct arose! While some might argue that women would still be second-class citizens without priestly ordination—the biblical scholar Elisabeth Schüssler Fiorenza has even argued that women should first be ordained to the episcopacy—nevertheless, for women to have the status and authority that ordination involves would mean that they would act in official capacities for the Church and be ministers of Word and Sacrament. Women would have *official* recognition of their service to the Church.

Anyone concerned about contemporary ministry, the role of women, and the future of the Church—that is, anyone concerned about the Church at all—is in the debt of Macy, Ditewig, and Zagano. This lucid and engaging book will open many eyes and hearts to the lost possibilities but also to the future promise of women's diaconal ministry. This book should be required reading for all bishops and clergy. Most of all, I hope that the millions of women involved in diaconal ministry in the Church today will read this book and take heart in the scholarship that these three gifted scholars have accomplished.

*Susan A. Ross*
*Loyola University Chicago*

# INTRODUCTION

The Catholic Church worldwide, as an institution and as the people of God, is suffering. While over a billion people call themselves "Catholic" and say they are members of the largest and most clearly identifiable organized religion on the planet, a large percentage of them suffer in too many ways. The recent implosion of the Church in Europe, preceded as it was by the explosion of scandals in the Americas, has damaged both the institutional Church universal and the individuals whose Christian beliefs are Catholic. The pity, of course, is that no one knows when it will end.

We do, however, know when it began. Christ himself warned of sinners among the flock, and things have not changed substantially since then. If history tells us anything, it tells us that the Church is both human and divine; when it follows the lead of the Spirit, it flourishes, and when it does not...it becomes corrupt and enters death throes. There is nothing new in the Church today that has not been seen many times before: the twin problems of sex and money are always ready to snake their ways into the lives of all of us, even into the very life of the Church.

It is against this backdrop, but independent of the problems, that we decided to take another look at the diaconate. We unabashedly hope in the future of the Church, and especially in the diaconate, the Church's engine of charity and heart of its ministry. Specifically, we wanted to look more closely, in a coordinated way, at women deacons. Our "look" eventually took shape as three related essays, one each from the perspective of our individual expertise.

The project plan was simple: Gary Macy would review the history of women in the diaconate; Bill Ditewig would examine the diaconate at present; and Phyllis Zagano would make suggestions for the inclusion of women as ordained deacons in the Catholic Church. The ground rules were simple: we were speaking about the diaconate, not about the priesthood. While we understood the separation, too many good folks do not, and that presented and presents difficulties in the discussion. Many people cannot "disconnect" the diaconate from the priesthood, simply because the diaconate in modern history has been only a "step" on the way to priesthood. That it has been restored as a permanent order does not seem to affect the misconception that deacons are "incomplete priests," or the idea that a deacon, once ordained, is automatically eligible for priestly ordination. Such is not the case, and it is important to state clearly at the outset: this book is not about women priests.

The history of the diaconate is long—arguably longer, even, than the history of the priesthood. We do not trace its development completely, but Gary Macy demonstrates that, as the diaconate grew, women were included. There is ample evidence of women deacons in the East from the earliest days of the Church to this day. We know women deacons existed early in the West as well. In fact, there is ample evidence of women deacons for over half of Christian history, until the twelfth century.

As the diaconate faded during the second millennium in the West, its remnants remained. For centuries, major Roman Catholic cathedrals had seven ceremonial deacons. Many fathers at the Council of Trent wanted to revive the diaconate, but failed. The cardinals of the Church (then and now) were ranked: cardinal bishop, priest, or deacon. Here and there a lay Vatican official was created a permanent deacon.[1] But the diaconate as a fully functioning separate and permanent order in the Roman Catholic Church did not begin to be restored until the end of the Second Vatican Council.

As the hierarchy considered the restoration of the diaconate as a permanent order, Pope Paul VI asked the perhaps-obvious question: What about women deacons? It is widely reported and believed that the positive answer he received was suppressed and remains unpublished as a Vatican document. But the research conducted by a member of the International Theological Commission, Cipriano Vagaggini, was published in *Orientalia Christiana Periodica*, the widely respected periodical published at the Pontifical Gregorian University in Rome, and edited by the famous professor of Eastern liturgy Robert F. Taft, SJ.[2] Vagaggini quite plainly stated that women were indeed ordained to the diaconate, by the bishop, within the sanctuary, with the laying on of hands. Vagaggini's article is not the only scholarship assessing the evidence for the ordination of women as deacons, but his is the only scholarship that points to a direct answer to a modern pope's inquiry: Were women ordained as deacons? The answer was yes.

By the time Vagaggini published his research, the issue of women's ordination to priesthood had exploded. The dust and smoke obscured the issue of women deacons as significant theological and popular discussion centered on women priests. Gradually the Catholic Church gave its answers regarding priests, first in a statement by the Congregation for the Doctrine of the Faith, *Inter Insigniores* (1976), and then with John Paul II's apostolic letter *Ordinatio Sacerdotalis* (1994). Each stated that the Church's constant tradition reserved priestly ordination to men alone. Neither addressed the question of women deacons.

Concurrently, various scholars were reviewing prior scholarship and evidence regarding women deacons. The discussion was twofold: Were women ever ordained deacons? Can women be ordained now? A famous debate in the 1970s between Roger Gryson and Aimé Georges Martimort left no resolution—Gryson said women were ordained; Martimort said they were not.[3] Yet it appears that their debate did not clearly separate the question of women deacons from the question of women priests.

By 2000, other studies and calls for women deacons appeared in the United States and Europe. Kyriaki Karidoyanes FitzGerald extended and expanded earlier work done by Evangelos Theodorou regarding the ordination of women deacons in Orthodoxy, and Phyllis Zagano made an argument for the restoration of the female diaconate for the entire Catholic Church, East and West.[4] Nearly concurrently, Ute Eisen published a review of the literary and epigraphical evidence of ordained women, including copious documentation about women deacons.[5] Later work by John Wijngaards argued for women as deacons as a step toward, or at least justification for, the ordination of women as priests.[6] Since then the question of women deacons has reappeared in various studies, notably in the historical work of Carolyn Oisek and Kevin Madigan and of Gary Macy.[7]

Meanwhile, the Church at large has never quite dismissed the notion of women deacons. Here and there, from the mid-1970s to the present, one or another bishop is said to have raised the question of women deacons during his *ad limina* visit to the pope. During the 1990s, groups as diverse as the Canon Law Society of America and the German-based We Are Church movement pressed the issue. In 2010, the

U.S.–based activist group FutureChurch initiated an international e-mail and postcard campaign to the Vatican (with copies to local bishops) in support of women deacons.

And so we have reentered the discussion about women deacons. To be clear, we are speaking about women ordained to what has come to be called the "permanent" diaconate. That is, we are not speaking about "deaconesses" as a fourth (and minor) order separate from the order of deacons. While history records both women called "deacons" and women called "deaconesses," we are not dependent upon history alone as the determinant of our views. Language regarding women's ministry in the Church fluctuates in the warp and woof of time: some women called "deaconess" were ordained to diaconal ministry; some women called "deaconess" were married to men deacons; and some women called "deaconess" merely appropriated (or were given) the name as a description for what they were doing. Of course, some of the wives of male deacons could themselves have been female deacons, and thus so titled. No matter the wavering terminology, it has become clear that in many parts of the Church, East and West, bishops formally appointed women to perform diaconal ministry, often through ceremonies we now recognize as ordinations.

We choose the term *woman deacon* (as opposed to *deaconess*) to highlight our interest in the genuine inclusion of women in the ordained ministry we now recognize as the diaconate. In considering terminology, we became involved in an interesting discussion with a number of scholars. The fact of the matter is this: If we say "woman deacon," are we perhaps indicating a sort of special case? That is, by saying "woman deacon," are we specifying that the ministry was only unusually filled by a woman? We think not, and this is our entire point. The historical diaconate was both male and female. Certain ministries were carried out by women who were deacons on behalf of other women. Men simply did not have (nor should have had) access to women at the baptismal font or in the sickbed due to propriety. A major part of the problem is the terminology we have become accustomed to in English. We do say "lady doctor" or "female pilot" or "woman preacher." At the end of it all, we determined that the term *woman deacon* would best indicate what we mean now: a woman who is ordained to the diaconate, to serve equally the ministry of the Word, the liturgy, and charity.

Of course, we could not do this without looking at the way the Second Vatican Council reinvigorated the diaconate as a permanent ministry, which now counts 35,000 ordained men (16,500 in the United States). Bill Ditewig traces the variety of ecclesial documents related to the renewed order of deacons, contextualizing them among similar documents related to the priesthood. He examines the diversity within the one sacrament of orders, a diversity clearly delineated in the official record. Given this diversity, which already admits of different practices between deacons and priests (such as permitting married men to be ordained deacons), one may ask, along with some council fathers, what other possibilities might exist, particularly whether women might be ordained as deacons.

Within this context, Ditewig also examines the Second Vatican Council's debate on the diaconate, especially an extensive conversation on the nature of sacramental grace as it applies to the Church in general and to the diaconate in particular. Grace, as divine gift, is given to the entire Church, and one of those graces is the diaconate itself. Similarly, Ditewig points out that two of the most influential players at the Council, Cardinal Suenens and Cardinal Döpfner, spoke of the fact that the sacramental grace of the sacrament of orders should be extended, through ordination, to those who are already exercising the functions of deacons. Their claim would apply to all who are exercising such functions, including women.

Yet, since the close of the Second Vatican Council, there has been no real movement on the part of the Vatican toward the restoration of the female diaconate in the Catholic Church, even as other recognized Churches (notably the Armenian Apostolic Church and the Orthodox Church of Greece) have retained or determined to restore their ancient tradition of women deacons. Movement in the Catholic Church, in fact, seems to seesaw. On the one hand, Pope Benedict XVI has called for the inclusion of women in Church *governance* and *ministry*. Each term has a specific formal meaning, especially for Benedict, a historical theologian and formerly long-term head of the Congregation for the Doctrine of the Faith. Only clerics (including deacons) can exercise governance and ministry. The use of such terms might point to papal interest in restoring women deacons, yet on the other hand, the Congregation for the Doctrine of the Faith first decreed and then codified the prohibition of the ordination of women to any grade of sacred order.

Even so, law is not doctrine, and the most recent official document treating the theology and history of the diaconate specifically leaves the question of women deacons open, stating that the question is to be resolved by the magisterium, but suggesting no timeline and giving no end date. And so we continue the discussion.

What if the diaconate *were* opened to women? What would it look like and how would it work? In the final essay here, Phyllis Zagano continues the discussion about the diaconate specifically as it applies to women. Some have suggested that there is no need for women deacons—that women serve and can serve in diaconal ways without ordination. Examining that suggestion, Zagano supposes the idea might be rooted in the denial of the efficacy of grace, particularly sacramental grace. She develops the theme and presents several other objections and complications to the possibility of women deacons.

She also notes the complicating fact that the predominance of diaconal ministry heretofore was performed by apostolic women religious, whose strength and influence are now fading. As institutes die out, she asks, is it possible that younger women seeking to serve the Church would be drawn instead to the ordained diaconate, just as might the large numbers of women already serving as lay ecclesial ministers (either as seculars or religious)? Further, Zagano examines the canonical stipulations regarding membership of clerics (which women deacons would be) in lay institutes.

The work here presented is a collaborative work. Each of us has read and commented on the others' essays in an effort to present a coherent and cogent discussion of this important issue in the Church. Overall, we are looking to the past and the present not so much to predict the future as, rather, to build it.

# WOMEN DEACONS: HISTORY

## Gary Macy

While a great deal of controversy exists concerning the ordination and function of women deacons in Christianity, there is little disagreement over their existence.[1] Study after study has investigated the evidence concerning women deacons in both the Eastern and Western Churches, leaving little doubt that women deacons existed for centuries in Christianity. Recently a number of collections of the relevant historical documents, often translated into modern languages, have been made available to a wider audience by Josephine Mayer;[2] Adriana Valerio;[3] Heike Grierser, Rosemarie Nürnberg, and Gisela Muschiol;[4] Ute Eisen;[5] Kyriaki Karidoyanes FitzGerald;[6] John Wijngaards;[7] and Kevin Madigan and Carolyn Osiek.[8] These collections and the wonderful studies done on women deacons starting with Jean Morin in the seventeenth century have made it clear that women served as deacons from the earliest centuries of Christianity and remained active in both the Eastern and Western Churches until the twelfth century.[9]

## SCRIPTURAL REFERENCES TO WOMEN DEACONS

The earliest reference to women as deacons appears in the Letter of Paul to the Romans:

9

> I commend to you our sister Phoebe, a deacon of
> the church at Cenchreae, so that you may welcome
> her in the Lord as is fitting for the saints, and help
> her in whatever she may require from you, for she
> has been a benefactor of many and of myself as
> well. (Rom 16:1–2)

Early Christian writers had no problem with a straightfor-
ward reading of this passage. Origen, writing in the third
century, simply stated, "This passage teaches by apostolic
authority that women also are appointed in the ministry of
the church, in which office Phoebe was placed at the church
that is in Cenchreae."[10] John Chrysostom and Theodoret of
Cyrrhus in the East and the anonymous Ambrosiaster and
Pelagius in the West also recognized Phoebe as a deacon in
their commentaries on Paul.[11]

Another passage from Scripture traditionally recognized as referring to women deacons is 1 Timothy 3:8–11:

> Deacons likewise must be serious, not double-
> tongued, not indulging in much wine, not greedy
> for money; they must hold fast to the mystery of
> the faith with a clear conscience. And let them first
> be tested; then, if they prove themselves blame-
> less, let them serve as deacons. Women likewise
> must be serious, not slanderers, but temperate,
> faithful in all things.

A number of early Church writers assumed that this passage
referred to the requirements for male deacons, followed by
the requirements for women deacons. John Chrysostom is
very clear: "Some say that he [Paul] is talking about women
in general, but that cannot be. Why would he want to insert

in the middle of what he is saying something about women? But rather, he is speaking of those women who hold the rank of deacon."[12] Clement of Alexandria,[13] Theodoret of Cyrrhus,[14] Theodore of Mopsuestia,[15] and Pelagius[16] joined John in his interpretation, with Theodore adding that "Paul does not wish to say this in this passage because it is right for such [deacons] to have wives; but since it is fitting for women to be established to perform duties similar to those of deacons."[17]

Not all writers agreed, of course. Ambrosiaster argued that only heretics would think that women deacons were meant in this passage.[18] He was in the minority, however, up until the thirteenth century, when his interpretation became the standard one in the West. For instance, during the twelfth century, Abelard, the famous and controversial scholar, would still understand both Romans 16 and 1 Timothy 3 to refer to women deacons, quoting not only Origen, but also Jerome (fourth century), Epiphanius (fourth century), Cassiodorus (sixth century), and Claudius of Turin (ninth century) to support his reading.[19] His famous student Gilbert of LaPorré followed Abelard in reading the Letters of Paul as referring to women deacons.[20]

It would seem, then, that these passages were understood by the majority of Christian scholars for over half of Christian history to refer to women who served as deacons in the Church. This would imply that during those centuries, the role of women as deacons was understood to have been sanctioned by Scripture and to have an apostolic foundation.

## WOMEN DEACONS IN THE EASTERN CHURCH

Christian (and non-Christian) writers refer to women deacons in the early Eastern Church. Dozens of references are witnessed by the collections mentioned above. In letters, lives of the saints, chronicles, inscriptions, and laws from the first through the sixth centuries, some forty different women are remembered and praised. Women were certainly active deacons and recognized as such in the Eastern Church.

Since women deacons were much more prevalent and therefore better known in the Eastern Church than in the Western Church, a few of the more outstanding examples should suffice to demonstrate how important they were. John Chrysostom wrote four letters to the woman deacon Amproukla in Constantinople, thanking her for her support while he was in exile.[21] Four letters survive to the woman deacon Anastasia from Severus, the bishop of Antioch, after he was exiled in 518. They corresponded on questions of scriptural exegesis, proving that Anastasia had a sophisticated knowledge of the Bible.[22] Theodoret of Cyrrhus wrote to the woman deacon Celerina in Constantinople, urging her to convince the bishops she knew of the orthodoxy of Theodoret's Christology.[23] Again, here is an influential and learned woman discussing complex theology with the most learned scholars of her day.

The most famous and influential of the women deacons, however, was certainly Olympias. Born into a wealthy and influential family, as a child she knew Gregory Nazianzus, who sent a poem as a gift when she wed the prefect of Constantinople, Nebridius, in 385. Nebridius died a year later and Olympias refused ever to remarry. She was ordained deacon by Bishop Nectarius while in her thirties and became his patron and political and personal advisor. Not only was an anonymous biography written shortly after her death, but she also appeared in the life of St. John Chrysostom and figured prominently as well in the important histories of the Church from that period.[24]

Women deacons continued to play a role in Eastern Christianity and are mentioned by several later texts. Headstones remain from the graves of several women deacons in the Eastern Church, dating from the fifth through the seventh centuries.[25] The Trullan Synod held in Constantinople in 692 decreed that women deacons should be at least forty years old before being ordained, indicating that they were still active in the Church.[26] According to the Canonical Collection of the Patriarch Photius of Constantinople, there were forty women deacons in that Church in the ninth century.[27] By the eleventh century, however, women deacons were no longer ordained in the Eastern Church, although later writers certainly knew of the early custom of having female deacons. From the earliest days of Christianity, then, and for over half of Christian history, women deacons played an important role in the Eastern Church and were remembered to have done so even after they no longer existed as an order in the Church.

## WOMEN DEACONS IN THE WESTERN CHURCH

References to women deacons as such in Western Christianity first appear with certainty in the fifth century, thus much later than in the Eastern Church. Ambrosiaster and Pelagius, as mentioned above, both referred to women deacons, but they understood this institution to be an Eastern practice, not one of their own Western Church. The Council of Nîmes in 394, noting that "women seemed to have been assumed into levitical service," ordered that "such ordination should be undone when it is effected contrary to reason. It should be seen that no one so presume in the future." Some scholars have argued that it was the diaconate itself that the Council intended to forbid.[28] The First Council of Orange, held in 441, certainly did know of women deacons and was not thrilled about them. "Women deacons are by no means to be ordained. If there are any who have already been ordained, let them submit their heads to the benediction that is granted to the people." It is very hard to know precisely which ministry the bishops were trying to proscribe here, since there is no other evidence for women deacons in the West during this early period. Is it possible that these women deacons were in fact from the East? Indeed, the Council of Nîmes in 394 had been concerned as well about "so-called priests and deacons coming from the far eastern parts" and decreed that they were not to be admitted to the ministry of the altar. One possibility, then, would be that women deacons first came to the West from the Eastern Churches.[29]

Another possibility is that the women in the West who played the same roles as women deacons in the East were called "widows" rather than deacons. Widows were also an order of women in the early Church, who had their own distinctive garb, vows, and place in church during the liturgy. The Council of Epaon, held in 517, for example, conflated the ministries of widow and woman deacon when the bishop there annulled throughout the region the consecration of widows "who are called women deacons."[30] Again it may be to such women that the Second Council of Orange addressed itself in 533: "Women who, up to this point, against its interdiction by the canons, received the benediction of the diaconate, if they be proven to have again entered into marriage, are to be banished from communion."[31] The council fathers then went on once again to attempt to abolish the office of woman deacon, justifying this decision on the basis of the fragility of women. As we will see later on, women deacons were required by canon law to remain continent even if they were married. Once they had taken a vow of continence, they could not remarry once they were widowed. For nearly one hundred years, the Merovingian bishops then continuously attempted to ban the order of women deacons in the West. Their ambition in this was notably frustrated as the following centuries witnessed a number of women who were ordained women deacons.

The references to particular women who were deacons in the Western Church are much less well known and are not included in most of the collections of documents mentioned above. There is a significant number, however, spread over seven centuries. Besides the documents from councils that we have already mentioned, there are a number of references in wills, letters, and chronicles of women who were deacons. Remigius, the long-lived bishop of Reims (ca. 433–ca. 533), left a will in which he bequeathed the servant named Noca and part of a vineyard to "my blessed daughter, Helaria the deaconess."[32]

The most famous woman deacon in the Western Church was certainly Queen Radegund, the wife of King Clothar I (511–58). She dramatically left the king in about 550 and demanded that she be ordained a deacon by Médard, bishop of Noyen, who, despite his fear of the king's retribution, reluctantly complied. Poet and bishop Venantius Fortunatus described the event vividly:

> She left the king and went straight to the holy Médard at Noyon. She earnestly begged that she might change her garments and be consecrated to God. But mindful of the words of the Apostle: "Art thou bound unto a wife? Seek not to be loosed," he hesitated to garb the Queen in the robe of a *monacha* [nun]. For even then, nobles were harassing the holy man and attempting to drag him brutally though the basilica from the altar to keep him from veiling the king's spouse lest the priest imagine he could take

away the king's official queen as though she were only a prostitute. The holiest of women knew this and, sizing up the situation, entered the sacristy [and] put on [the Queen] a monastic garb and [she] proceeded straight to the altar, saying to the blessed Médard: "If you shrink from consecrating me, and fear man more than God, Pastor, He will require His sheep's soul from your hand." He was thunderstruck by that argument and, laying his hand on her, he consecrated her as deaconess.[33]

Inscriptions have left us much briefer memorials to three other women deacons: Anna, a woman deacon from Rome in the sixth century; Theodora, a woman deacon from Gaul buried in 539; and Ausonia, a woman deacon from Dalmatia in the sixth century. The inscription to Ausonia mentioned her children, thus making her as the only one of these three with evidence that she was married. In the second half of the seventh century, the anonymous author of the life of St. Sigolena described how she was consecrated a deacon (*consecravit diaconam*) after the death of her husband. In a charter from 636, Deacon Grimo of Trier referred to his sister Emengaud as a deacon.[34]

A number of references to women deacons also exist from the eighth century. Pope Gregory II wrote three letters to women deacons between 715 and 730. Two are addressed to the women deacons of St. Eustachius and one to Matrona, a religious woman deacon, and her sons and nephews.[35] A prohibition by Pope Zachary in 743 proclaimed that "no one should presume to join himself physically to an abominable consort, like a *presbytera* [the Latin term for a woman priest], woman deacon, nun or female monk or a godmother."[36] Sergius, after becoming archbishop of Ravenna in 753, "consecrated his wife, Euphemia, a deacon (*diaconissa*)."[37] When Leo III returned to Rome in 799, a chronicle of the event mentioned that he was greeted by the entire population, including "holy women, women deacons (*diaconissae*) and the most noble matrons."[38] The Council of Rome, held in 826, forbade certain illegal marriages, including those with any veiled woman or woman deacon.[39] Women deacons continued to appear in documents between the tenth and twelfth centuries. Pope Leo VII (c. 937–39) repeated the prohibition of the Council of Rome from 826, and the ninth-century collection of laws known as the Pseudo-Isidorian Decretals similarly forbade the marriage of women deacons.[40]

In 1018, Benedict VIII conferred on the cardinal bishop of Porto the right to ordain bishops, priests, male or female deacons (*diaconibus vel diaconissis*), subdeacons, churches, and altars. This privilege was again granted by John XIX in 1025 and by Leo IX in 1049. In 1026, John XIX conceded to the bishop of Silva Candida[41] "consecrations of the altar of the church of St. Peter and of other monasteries, also the consecration of churches, altars, priests, clerics, deacons, or deaconesses for the whole Leonine City."[42] Benedict IX continued this privilege in 1037.[43] Women deacons existed in the diocese of Lucca in Italy at least up until the time of Ottone, bishop from 1139 to 1146.[44] The famous twelfth-century theologian Abelard and his wife Heloise, writing in France, both referred to her status as a deacon.[45]

Even more important than the references to women deacons in the literature of the first twelve hundred years of Christianity is the existence of the liturgy for the ordination of women as deacons. Along with the rituals for the ordination of bishops, priests, and deacons, the books used by bishops for religious ceremonies also include the services for women deacons.

# ORDINATION RITES FOR WOMEN DEACONS IN THE EASTERN CHURCH

The rites for the ordination of women as deacons appear very early in Christianity. One of the earliest prayers for such a ceremony appears in a collection of Church Orders complied from earlier materials and now known as the *Apostolic Constitutions*:

> But now concerning a deaconess, I Bartholomew make this teaching. O, bishop, you will lay your hands on her in the presence of the presbyters and the deacons and you will say: "O, Eternal God, the father of our Lord, Jesus Christ, Creator of man and woman, who filled with the Spirit Miriam and Deborah and Anna and Huldah, who did not disdain that your only begotten son should be born of a woman, who also in the tabernacle of testimony and in the Temple appointed the guardians of the holy gates, now also look upon your servant who is to be appointed to the diaconate and give her the holy Spirit and cleanse her from all filthiness of flesh and spirit that she may worthily perform the work which is entrusted to your glory and the praise of your Christ, with whom glory and worship be to you and the holy Spirit for ever. Amen.[46]

In 1655, the great seventeenth-century liturgist Jean Morin produced a monumental collection of ordination rites in Greek, Latin, and Syriac. He included a separate section discussing women deacons and concluded that the same rites were used for deacons and women deacons in the most ancient Greek rituals.[47]

Three of the most ancient Greek rituals, uniformly
one in agreement, hand down to us the ordination
of women deacons, administered by almost the
same rites and words by which deacons [were
ordained]. Both are called ordination, χειρτονία,
χειροφεσία. Both are celebrated at the altar by the
bishop, and in the same liturgical space. Hands are
placed on both while the bishop offers prayers.
The stole is placed on the neck of both, both the
ordained man and the ordained woman communi-
cate, the chalice full of the blood of Christ placed in
the hands of both so they may taste of it.[48]

John Wijngaards came to a similar conclusion in his
study of the ten oldest manuscripts containing the Greek ritual for the ordination of women deacons. These date from
the eighth through the fourteenth centuries. He provides an
analysis and translation into English of the ordination
prayers.[49] Kyriaki Karidoyanes FitzGerald also analyzes and
translates the eighth century ceremony for the ordination of
a woman deacon. In Dr. FitzGerald's translation, the prayer
of ordination reads:

Holy and Omnipotent Lord, through the birth of
your Only Son our God from a Virgin according to
the flesh, you have sanctified the female sex. You
grant not only to men, but also to women the grace
and coming of the Holy Spirit. Please, Lord, look on
this your maidservant and dedicate her to the task
of your diaconate, and pour out into her the rich
and abundant giving of your Holy Spirit. Preserve
her so that she may always perform her ministry
with orthodox faith and irreproachable conduct,

according to what is pleasing to you. For to you is
due all glory and honor.[50]

It is clear from this evidence that women were continuously ordained deacons in the Eastern Church for many centuries. There are references to women who were deacons
throughout this period, and the liturgies to ordain women to
this function exist from the fourth through the fourteenth
centuries.

## ORDINATION RITES FOR WOMEN DEACONS
## IN THE WESTERN CHURCH

The earliest rituals in the West for the ordination of a
woman deacon come from the eighth-century liturgical book
of Bishop Egbert of York.[51] The book contains a single prayer
for the ordaining of either a male or a female deacon, which
appears in the middle of the ordination rite for a deacon. The
impression given is that the ordination rite for a male deacon
is the same as that used for a female deacon. This prayer will
appear often in rituals for both male and female deacons and
constitutes the most frequent prayer of consecration for this
office. The prayer reads: "Give heed, Lord, to our prayers and
upon this your servant send forth that spirit of your blessing
in order that, enriched by heavenly gifts, he [or she] might be
able to obtain grace through your majesty and by living well
offer an example to others. Through [our Lord Jesus
Christ]."[52]

Egbert's pontifical also contains separate prayers for the
blessing of a female and a male deacon. They differ substantially. The prayer over a woman deacon stresses her virginity,
referring to the wise virgins who waited for the bridegroom

with the oil of virtue. The prayer over male deacons begs God for peace and prosperity, promising the blessing of God on the image that God formed in him.

The ninth-century Gregorian sacramentary gives precisely the same prayer for the making of a female deacon as does the pontifical of Egbert: "Give heed, O Lord." The prayer appears again as an alternate prayer in the ceremony for the ordaining of a deacon. In this case, the prayer for the making of a woman deacon appears separately from the ordination rite for deacon. As no complete ceremony is given for the ordination of a woman deacon, it seems that the same ritual was used for the ordaining of a male deacon and of a woman deacon. There would be no reason to repeat the entire ritual for both offices unless they were different. Only the ordination prayer would need to be included as a separate item, as indeed it is.

The tenth-century Romano-Germanic Pontifical contains the complete liturgy for both the ordination of a woman deacon and the ordination of a male deacon. The ordination rite for a woman deacon takes place within the Mass and begins with the instructions, "When the bishop blesses the deaconess, he places the orarium on her neck. However, when she proceeds to the church, she wears it around her neck so that the ends on both sides of the orarium are under her tunic."[53] The *orarium* is a form of stole that, according to the Council of Toledo in 633, was worn by bishops, priests, and deacons. According to this Council, the deacon was to wear his *orarium* on his left side when he "prayed, that is preached."[54] The *orarium* would be one of the instruments of the woman deacon, indicating her function, which in this case would be preaching. This would make sense in light of the ninth-century canonical commentaries that describe women deacons as "ordained through the

21

imposition of hands by a bishop...in order to instruct all Christian women in the faith and law of God, as they did in the old law."[55] Following the Gradual (a prayer between the first reading of the liturgy and the Gospel reading),[56] the woman deacon prostrates herself before the bishop during the litany, after which he recites the prayer "Give heed, O Lord." The directions for the ritual continue with a prayer of consecration that strongly emphasizes the chastity of the woman deacon, comparing her to Anna, the widow mentioned in Luke 2:36–38, and indeed this prayer had been used in early sacramentaries as a consecration prayer for widows. According to the prayer, the office of female deacon was instituted by the apostles for the instruction of young women. The woman deacon is to be anointed with chrism by the hand of the bishop.

The bishop then places the *orarium* around the neck of the woman deacon, calling it a *stola*, the same word used for the stole of deacon. Because in the rite for a priest in the same sacramentary the stole is called an *orarium*, the two terms seem to be interchangeable. The woman deacon herself takes a veil from the altar and places it on her own head. Finally, the woman deacon accepts a ring and a crown from the bishop. The reception of the veil, the ring, and the crown—but not the stole—are also part of the ritual used in the consecration of virgins.

An almost identical liturgy appears as well in the twelfth-century Roman Pontifical. This version, however, is without instructions, so it is difficult to know exactly how the ritual proceeded. Further, the prayer "Give heed, O Lord" does not appear. However, the fact that the liturgy was included in the pontifical is important. Also, according to the famous liturgical historian Cyrille Vogel, "The Roman liturgists aimed at eliminating a good deal of archaic and unnecessary material from the Mainz Pontifical [the Romano-Germanic Pontifical]....The rites that were retained were either simplified...or adapted to the peculiar conditions of the Church of Rome."[57] This would indicate that the rite was indeed used in the papal city into the twelfth century. The ordination ceremony for the ordination of a woman deacon was dropped in the thirteenth-century Roman Pontifical and does not appear again. Not surprising, the twelfth century also contains the last reference to a woman deacon, Heloise of Paris. By the thirteenth century, this office had disappeared from the Western Church.

So women deacons were there, working in both the Eastern and Western Churches for centuries before slowly disappearing from the scene around the twelfth century. Historians are sure they were there; they are not so certain about what they did.

## THE MINISTRY OF WOMEN DEACONS

In the early years of Christianity, women who were designated deacons probably did the same thing that men designated as deacons did. *Diakonos* in Greek just means "servant," and so the "servants" of the Church did the service jobs. They took care of the poor, visited the sick and those in prison, and generally looked to the upkeep of the fabric of the Church. It probably wasn't an "order" in the way we think of it at all. It was a job description; these were the people chosen by the community to handle what we might call "social services." This was a big job, because there were very few such services in the Roman Empire, apart from the Jewish community from which Christianity got its social ethic. In fact, according to the historian of the early Church Henry Chadwick, the charity of the Christians was probably the reason for their great success in drawing converts.[58]

The first reference to the role of service that would become the hallmark of deacons[59] is described in the Acts of the Apostles:

> Now during those days, when the disciples were increasing in number, the Hellenists complained against the Hebrews because their widows were being neglected in the daily distribution of food. And the twelve called together the whole community of the disciples and said, "It is not right that we should neglect the word of God in order to wait on tables. Therefore, friends, select from among yourselves seven men of good standing, full of the Spirit and of wisdom, whom we may appoint to this task, while we, for our part, will devote ourselves to prayer and to serving the word." (Acts 6:1–4)

Not surprisingly, care of sick women and of poor women was undertaken by women chosen by the Christian community for this task. They were called "deacons" because that is the role they played. In the fourth-century *Apostolic Constitutions*, one finds this role carefully spelled out: "And let the woman [deacon] be diligent in taking care of the women. Both of them [male and female deacons] should be ready to carry messages, to travel about, to minister, and to serve."[60] Later on in the section of the *Constitutions* known as the Apostolic Canons, the role of women as ministers to the sick is specifically mentioned: "The other one [of three women chosen] will look after the women who are suffering illnesses. She should be a good deacon, reliable, reporting whatever is needed to the priests, not given to wine, not greedy for money (from 1 Tim. 3:8), so that she can stay awake at night, or if someone else asks her to do other good works."[61]

Women deacons also preached the Gospel to other women, going into places where men were not allowed. Clement of Alexandria, writing in the second century, described this role:

> But the [apostles], in accordance with their ministry, devoted themselves to preaching without any distraction, and took women with them, not as wives, but as sisters, that they might be their co-ministers in dealing with women in their homes. It was through them that the Lord's teaching penetrated also the women's quarters without any scandal being aroused. We also know the instructions about women deacons which are given by the noble Paul in his other letter, the one to Timothy (1 Tim. 3:11).[62]

The teaching role of women seems to have continued at least into the fourth century, when Pelagius noted that "in the eastern regions one sees women deaconesses [*diaconissae mulieres*], even to this day, serving members of their own sex in baptism and in the ministry of the word. For we find women who teach in private, as did Priscilla whose husband was called Aquila."[63]

Gradually, just as did the male deacons, women deacons acquired liturgical roles as well. Most importantly, they undressed and led the female catechumens into the baptistery font. Out of modesty, of course, this was something the male deacons could not do. The *Apostolic Constitutions* explained: "For we stand in need of a woman deacon for many reasons, first in the baptism of women, the male deacon will anoint only their foreheads with holy oil and after him, the female deacon shall anoint them; for there is no necessity for the women to be seen by the men."[64]

In at least the Western Church, there are references to women deacons reading the Gospel. As we have already seen, women deacons received the orarium (stole) when they were ordained in the West. This garment was specifically meant to be worn when preaching. A woman also received this garment in the Eastern liturgies after the ordination and before she received communion.[65]

Also, in at least the West, the memory of women deacons reading the Gospel lasted into the twelfth century. A massive collection of Church laws compiled by the monk Gratian in Bologna in the mid-twelfth century soon became the standard text both for the teaching and the implementation of Church law. The *Decretum*, as it was commonly known, was the basis for much of Roman Catholic Church law until it was revised in 1917. The influential scholar Rolandus, commenting on the *Decretum* around 1148, agreed that "there is no doubt that it was the custom in the past to ordain women deacons, that is, readers of the Gospel, who were not to be ordained before forty years of age, nor were they allowed to be married after ordination."[66] Stephen of Tournai (writing in the 1160s) copied Rolandus, suggesting that these holy women were called women deacons because they were permitted to read the Gospel. Later canonists, such as the influential scholars Huguccio of Bologna and Johannes Teutonicus (John the German), would argue that the women deacons had never truly been ordained at all, but they still granted that some women may have been called deacons because they received a special blessing that allowed them to read the Gospel, although not at Mass.[67] So it seems quite likely that women deacons did read the Gospel in the early Middle Ages, and in fact that was considered their main function as deacons.

## MARRIED WOMEN DEACONS

It seems that at least in the early Middle Ages, some women deacons may have been married,[68] although there is only one explicit reference to this. The Second Council of Tours in 567 forbade women deacons from sleeping with their husbands, who were also called deacons. There are many more references to the wives of bishops and priests who are called *presbytera* (women priests) and *episcopa* (women bishops). It seems that some but not all women deacons belonged to a group of women whose husbands were also clergy. The wives of bishops, priests, and deacons were obliged by Church law to separate from their husbands and live lives of continence similar to those of widows, virgins, or nuns. Both spouses mutually agreed to enter into such an arrangement. The Councils of Orange in 441, of Agde in 506, of Arles in 524, and of Toledo in 633 all called such a mutual decision a "conversion" or "profession," common terms for entering a religious order. As late as the mid-eleventh century, as required by Pope Leo IX, the consent of both spouses was needed before a minor cleric could become a subdeacon. In effect, both parties were expected to enter the religious, vowed life. Once women entered this *ordo*, they were, in practice if not in reality, widows. At the Council of Gérone in 517, spouses were encouraged to live in separate houses, and at the Council of Lyon in 583, spouses were enjoined even not to share daily activities. Several councils punished priests who fathered children or punished those who returned to their wives for conjugal relations. Some couples were at least described as living in separate establishments.

Not all bishops, priests, and deacons separated from their wives or undertook a life of continence, however. According to Jo Ann McNamara: "These clerical proponents of the chaste marriage were, however, an elite. They provided an example that could hardly have been expected to suit the vast majority of the clergy."[69] Clergy continued to marry and live active married lives well into the twelfth century. If there were ceremonies whereby the wives of priests or deacons took on vows and a life of continence, perhaps only those women who separated from their husbands and underwent such a ceremony were called *episcopae, presbyterae*, and *diacona* or *diaconissa*. If so, then some, but again not all, women deacons were the wives of deacons who took vows of continence.

This does not mean that these women did not perform the regular ministry of a deacon. In fact, a married couple may have formed a "pastoral team" in which they performed diaconal duties together. Since there is evidence, as already described, that women deacons taught other women, prepared them for baptism, and read the Gospel at Mass, there is no reason to think that all of these functions were performed by women deacons who were married. Both husband and wife would have been deacons who also took an extra vow of continence in their marriage.

## ABBESSES AS WOMEN DEACONS

In the Western Church abbesses were sometimes deacons. Radegund and Sigolena, for example, were ordained as deacons but also became abbesses.[70] A group of ninth- and tenth-century commentators on canon law presumed that abbesses were deacons, simply stating, "A female deacon is an abbess."[71] Similarly, Atto, bishop of Vercelli (ca. 924–ca. 960), spoke of writers who claimed that women called "deacons" in the past were now named "abbesses." It seems that over time, abbesses came to be understood as the living continuation of the ancient ministry of woman deacons founded by the apostles.

In this sense, then, in the eyes of the medievals, women deacons did not die out in the West. They continued to function in the Church continuously from the time of Christ. It is easy to understand why contemporaries might have held this opinion. Abbesses did many things women deacons had done. They read the Gospel. They sometimes distributed communion. They certainly taught young women and sometimes taught young men. In this sense, women deacons lived on long after the specific name had faded from the ecclesiastical scene, in so far as abbesses continued to perform diaconal functions among their many other duties.

Several twelfth-century canonists, as mentioned above, referred to abbesses as the "new" female deacons, but it was the twelfth-century theologian Abelard who most passionately and learnedly defended the position that holy women (*sanctimonialia*) constituted an ancient order of the Church and, more specifically, that abbesses were now women deacons. He wrote on this subject several times, but his most extended defense came at the instigation of his wife, the abbess Heloise, who referred to herself as a deacon (*diaconissa*). She requested that Abelard produce a history of her order of holy women (*sanctimonialia*). Abelard responded with possibly the most thorough and passionate defense of the ordination of women in the High Middle Ages.[72] Abelard's response to Heloise's request for a history of and justification for women's orders has been described by both Jean

Leclercq and Mary Martin McLaughlin as "unique in medieval literature."[73]

Abelard repeatedly and pointedly asserted that the title "abbess" was the new name for the ancient order of women deacons. The identification of abbesses as the successors of the women deacons of the early Church so thoroughly dominated Abelard's and Heloise's thought that both used the title "deacon" interchangeably with the title "abbess." Heloise and Abelard quoted sources that referred to deacons/abbesses both as ordained and as an order. Both Abelard and Heloise considered abbesses to be the successors to the ancient order of women deacons, an ordained clerical office established by Christ himself. Abelard's repeated defense of this position could not be clearer; even the way in which Heloise phrased her request to her husband suggests that this is precisely the position that she wished him to defend. In the words of McLaughlin, "[Abelard] could hardly, it seems, have gone to greater lengths in his quest for arguments, testimonies and examples that would exalt and dignify both the sex and the vocation of religious women."[74]

## THE DISAPPEARANCE OF WOMEN DEACONS

Abelard and Heloise were two of the last Christian writers in either the East or the West to argue for the continued existence of women in the diaconate. By the twelfth century, it seems that women deacons were a rarity in Eastern Christianity. Theodore Balsamon, the twelfth-century Greek canonist, remembered that there were once women deacons, but said that they no longer existed:

> In times past, orders (*tagmata*) of deaconesses were recognized, and they had access to the sanctuary

(*bema*). But the monthly affliction banished them
from the divine and holy sanctuary. In the holy
see of Constantinople, women deacons were
appointed to the office, without any participation
in the sanctuary, but attending to church functions
and directing women's assembly according to
church procedure.[75]

Theodore, however, did recognize that the title of woman
deacon still existed among some nuns, but they were not
ordained, again because of menstruation:

A deaconess (*diakonissa*) today is not ordained,
even if some female ascetics are loosely referred
to as deacons. For there is a canon that defines
that women may not enter the sanctuary. How
could one who cannot approach the altar perform
the function of the deacon?[76]

The fourteenth-century canonist Matthew Blastares also
conceded that women once served as deacons, but this was
eventually forbidden, again because of menstruation:

Women deacons then fulfilled a certain service
among the clergy (*kleroi*), which is nearly unknown
to everyone now. There are some who say that
they baptized women because it was not proper
for men to see undressed those being baptized
who were of a certain age. Others say that they
were allowed to approach the holy altar and perform nearly all the functions done by male deacons.
They were forbidden access and performance of
these services by later fathers because of their

monthly flow that cannot be controlled. So it was legitimate in previous times for women to have access to the holy altar, and indeed for many to seek after it, especially according to the funeral oration that the great Gregory [Nazianzus] did for his sister.[77]

The argument against the ordination of female deacons given by Theodore and Matthew is very important. It seems that the major reason women stopped being ordained deacons in both the East and West was the gradual introduction of purity laws from the Hebrew Scriptures. Menstruation and childbirth were seen as impediments to women serving at the altar or to their eventually being ordained. The situation was slightly more complicated in the West because a letter from Pope Gregory I (590–604) proclaimed that menstruation should not be considered an obstacle to women attending church. Gradually, however, the purity laws won out, and women were considered unfit for ordination. Coupled with this legal argument was a radical change in the definition of ordination in the West, which gradually also influenced the East.[78]

The understanding of ordination before the eleventh-century reform movement in the Western Church was quite different from that which would emerge from the twelfth-century Scholastic and canonical debates.[79] For the first millennium of Christianity, the words *ordo* ("order"), *ordinatio* ("an ordering"), and *ordinare* ("to order") had far different meanings from those that they would come to have in later centuries. Christian communities appropriated the language of "ordination" from everyday usage. *Ordo* most commonly referred simply to one's state of life, and *ordinare* originally meant to provide order either in a political or a metaphoric sense. In fact, *ordinare* in its base meaning simple indicates some method of organization. To put your books in alphabetical order is, in Latin, "to ordain" them, and the act of so doing is an "ordination." *Ordines* (the plural of *ordo*) can also be a reference to the jobs in a certain group or society because that would be the way that group or society organized itself. Within the Christian community, of course, there were different jobs to do. These were naturally called *ordines*, and the process by which one was chosen for such a job was called *ordinatio*. Any job or vocation was called an *ordo*, and the process by which one was chosen and designated for that vocation was an ordination.

To quote Cardinal Yves Congar, a Church historian:

> Ordination encompassed at the same time election as its starting point and consecration as its term. But instead of signifying, as happened from the beginning of the twelfth century, the ceremony in which an individual received a power henceforth possessed in such a way that it could never be lost, the words *ordinare*, *ordinari*, *ordinatio* signified the fact of being designated and consecrated to take up a certain place, or better a certain function, *ordo*, in the community and at its service.[80]

Ordination did not give a person, for instance, the irrevocable and portable power of consecrating the bread and wine, or of leading the liturgy; rather, a particular community charged a person or persons to play a leadership role within that community (and only within that community) and that person or persons would lead the liturgy because of the leadership role they played within the community.

As the quotation from Yves Congar indicates, only in the twelfth and thirteenth centuries did theologians and canon-

ists devise, after lengthy debates, another definition of ordination. According to this definition—the one with which we
are most familiar today—ordination granted the recipient,
not a position within a community, but a power able to be
exercised in any community. In fact, according to the thirteenth-century theologians, ordination bestowed an indelible character on the souls of the ordained that marked them
as different from other Christians. The central power that
ordination granted was the power to consecrate the bread
and wine at the altar, and so, over time, ordination was considered to include only those *ordines* that served at the
altar—that is, the orders of priest, deacon, and subdeacon.
All of the other earlier orders were no longer considered to
be orders at all.[81]

As a part of this redefinition, women were excluded
from all the orders, including that of priest, deacon, and subdeacon. In fact, it was taught and believed, and still is held in
some quarters, that women never performed any of the roles
now limited to those three orders.

As we said earlier, commentary on the massive collection of Church law known as the *Decretum* mentioned
women's past roles as deacons. But the *Decretum* itself,
reflecting the new definition of ordination, stated that women
could not be deacons. Gratian completed the first recension of
the *Decretum* before the 1130s. The second recension, ca.
1150, became the standard textbook for canon law schools
throughout Western Europe, and formed Latin Church law at
least until the Reformation. In *causa* 15, *questio* 3, Gratian
posed the question whether a woman could give testimony in
a case against a priest. He answered that she could not give
such testimony, since "those who are not in the same *ordo*
cannot accuse nor testify against a priest, nor are they able to
do so. Women are not able to advance to the priesthood or

even to the diaconate, therefore they are capable of neither accusing priests nor of testifying against them."[82] This was the first clear and unambiguous statement that women could not be ordained either as priests or as deacons.

Despite this, the situation in the second half of the twelfth century in the West was still in flux: theologians were divided in their understanding of ordination, and canonists were deeply engaged in a discussion about the ordination of women deacons. While the *Decretum* said that women could not be ordained, it did include laws that *referred* to women deacons. The canonists were the first to discuss in depth what those references could possibly mean if women could not, in fact, "advance...even to the diaconate," as Gratian had claimed. The majority of the twelfth-century canonists followed Gratian in arguing that women could not be ordained, but the references presented an inherent problem with this position. Interestingly, the references come not from the Western Church, but from the East. *Causa* 27, *questio* 1, *caput* 23 of the *Decretum* quoted a law from the Council of Chalcedon of 451 that requires women deacons to be forty years of age and celibate. Two other references to women deacons are from the sixth-century *Novellae* of Justinian.[83]

These references kept alive the memory of women deacons and in doing so required that canonists somehow explain their existence. Some of the early canonists argued that women had indeed once been ordained deacons, but now abbesses should be considered deacons. Others, however, distinguished between "real" ordination, which was ordination to service at the altar, and an ordination that was really just a commissioning for a particular ministry. The "ordination" of women deacons, or of abbesses, was clearly of the second, nonsacramental variety. Such a distinction assumed a far different understanding of ordination from that used in earlier centuries. For in that early understanding, as we have seen, all ordinations were commissions to a particular ministry, not just those to the altar.[84]

Writing at the end of the twelfth century, the most influential canonist of his age, Huguccio of Bologna, went further than any of his predecessors in arguing that women could not be ordained. "But I say that a woman is not able to receive orders. What impedes this? The law of the church and sex, that is, the law of the church made on account of sex [impedes it]. If therefore a female is in fact ordained, she does not receive orders, and hence is forbidden to exercise the office of orders."[85] In other words, even if a woman were to be ordained, it would not "take." The mere fact of being a woman would negate any effect that an ordination might have. Despite opposition from Abelard and a few other writers, twelfth-century writers moved from conceding that women were once ordained, to teaching that women never were ordained, to teaching, finally, that women never could and never would be ordained. This final position is what canon lawyers and theologians would teach for the rest of the Middle Ages.

Within roughly a century, women lost all standing as ordained clergy. They could not be ordained even if they underwent a ceremony of ordination. They had never been truly ordained, despite any authorities to the contrary. All women were now simply laity, and further, they had always been laity and would always be laity. It was metaphysically impossible for them to be ordained, to have been ordained, or to ever be ordained. The ancient and centuries-old tradition of women deacons had come to a close.

# WOMEN DEACONS:
# PRESENT POSSIBILITIES
## William T. Ditewig

## INTRODUCTION

We shift our focus now from the historical to the theological. Evidence from history alone is not dispositive of the theological and pastoral question at hand: namely, can and should women be ordained as deacons? As we have seen, the historical record is quite illustrative on two major points: (1) ministry, including ordained ministry, was complex and varied in the ancient and medieval Church; and (2) women were there in the middle of things. Professor Macy's work has highlighted something else critically important for us. The historical record demonstrates that the theological meaning of what the Church has *meant* by ordination has shifted over time. That the Church's understanding of orders develops over time should not surprise us, and the history of the twentieth century shows us that another shift in understanding is taking place.

I am referring. namely, to the restructuring of the sacrament of orders following the Second Vatican Council. In this theological development that followed the Second Vatican Council, it is possible to see a *novus mentis habitus*—a new way of thinking—about ordained ministry. Among other things, conciliar decisions led to the complete restructuring of the sacrament of orders: in the West, the suppression of first tonsure; the suppression of the four minor orders of porter, lector, exorcist, and acolyte; and the suppression of the major order of subdiaconate. We now have a renewed diaconate, which is permanently exercised, and which is open to married as well as celibate men.

The nature and role of the episcopacy also came under scrutiny and renewal at Vatican II. All of this development has resulted in significant theological and canonical examination of the issues involved with this "new way of thinking" about ordained ministry. The theological understanding that emerged in the twelfth century, which Professor Macy has ably documented, is now itself in transition, as the Church gains experience with the renewed order of deacon and other new forms of official ministry. In this essay, then, I wish to touch upon some of those issues that may help address the question of the possibility of the ordination of women as deacons. Obviously, a full examination of these matters is beyond the scope of this project. I hope merely to sketch what I believe are important parameters for considering the question.

I have titled this essay "Present Possibilities." Given the state of theological reflection on the sacrament of orders in the contemporary Church, what is possible? Are critics who worry that we can't even discuss the question of women as deacons correct in their concerns? Others maintain that ordaining women as deacons would simply open the door to ordaining women as presbyters. And other critics say that considering women as deacons doesn't go far enough, because, in their opinion, the real question is about ordaining women as presbyters.

This essay aims to remain focused on the merits of this one very specific question: Is it possible, based on an examination of Church teaching and the vision of the Second Vatican Council vis-à-vis the diaconate, to ordain women as deacons? Ours is a worthy and legitimate question, although this is an emotional issue for many people who fear it. This question is examined with great respect for the Church and our tradition. This is not an act of defiance, which is how some people might interpret it, but rather of enthusiastic commitment to the best our tradition has to offer to the Church and world of our time.

We shall proceed in several steps. First, I shall consider the paradigm shift in the theology of the sacrament of orders wrought by Vatican II's renewal of a diaconate permanently exercised. With this decision and its implementation, it was again possible—after more than a millennium—to ordain someone to a major order of ministry *other than* the presbyterate. This was a stunning development! After all, to speak of "ordination" throughout the second millennium was to speak ultimately about the presbyterate. Even the 1917 Code of Canon Law instructed bishops, "First tonsure and orders are to be conferred only on those who are proposed for ascending to the presbyterate and who seem correctly understood as, at some point in the future, being worthy priests" (ca. 973).[1]

Second, I shall return to the Second Vatican Council and examine the thinking of the council fathers about the possibilities of a renewed diaconate. What vision did they have of this order? Why did they feel it was necessary to take this bold step? What might this vision suggest to us in our quest for answers to our question? Third, I shall conclude this study by turning, finally, to the question at hand. Given a new way of thinking about the nature of the diaconate as renewed by Vatican II and then the 1983 Code of Canon Law, what might we find about ordaining women deacons in the contemporary Church?

## DIACONATE AS A "PROPER AND PERMANENT ORDER" DISTINCT FROM PRIESTHOOD[2]

We begin with the opening words of paragraph 29 of Vatican II's *Dogmatic Constitution on the Church*:

> At a lower level of the hierarchy are deacons, who receive the imposition of hands "not unto priesthood, but unto service." For, strengthened by sacramental grace they are dedicated to the People of God, in conjunction with the bishop and his body of priests, in service of the liturgy, of the Word, and works of charity.[3]

The ancient assertion that deacons are not ordained to priesthood but to service has remained consistent throughout the history of the diaconate, while the cultural, canonical, and theological contexts within which this claim has been made have varied greatly. We take this statement at its word: deacons are not ordained to priesthood. A significant difficulty exists in understanding the contemporary diaconate as a "proper and permanent"[4] order in its own right precisely because much of the theological and canonical language that has developed concerning the ordained ministries emerged subsequent to the decline of the diaconate as a permanent order. While it is sometimes said that the diaconate had largely *disappeared* by the beginning of the second millennium, and that it was *restored* by the Second Vatican Council, these characterizations are inadequate in that they miss a significant paradigm shift. The diaconate *never* disappeared; rather, it was transformed and redefined into a transitory stage on the way to ultimate ordination into the presbyterate.

The Scholastic and modern development of the Church's understanding of official ministry, and of ordained ministry in particular, took place after the disappearance of the diaconate as a proper and permanent order, and prior to its renewal. This means that the predominant understanding of ordination has been almost exclusively *sacerdotal*. How a person may be sacramentally ordained yet not be in the priesthood is an idea that has been largely unexamined.

Both in history and theology, then, the diaconate ceased being described in its own terms and began to be defined and described by its relationship to the presbyterate, its ultimate end. The paradigm for discussions of ordained ministry, therefore, has been primarily sacerdotal and, in particular, presbyteral ministry. Other ministries, including the episcopate and diaconate—as well as various forms of lay ecclesial ministry—are often still measured against this paradigm.[5] Using such a frame of reference, ministries other than the presbyterate are often described in terms of what they are not: The laity are described as "nonordained." Deacons are described as men who "do not" say Mass, "do not" hear confessions, "do not" give last rites. This method of negative identification must be overcome if the diaconate is to develop into the "proper and permanent" order described by the Council.

*Lumen gentium* 29 and its implementation create a new challenge for sacramental theology. While the diaconate is to function in communion with the presbyterate, it has an identity unique in itself. Contemporary attempts in theology and canon law to define and describe the nature and functions of the diaconate must be examined critically so that language that may legitimately apply to the sacerdotal orders of bishop and presbyter is not applied inappropriately to the deacon. Therefore, since the diaconate is an ordained ministry in its own right, language unique to the order, and legal expressions flowing from that language, must continue to develop. The late canonist James H. Provost, who taught for many years at the Catholic University of America in Washington, DC, made the following observation about the diaconate as it appears in the 1983 Code of Canon Law: "There is still no coherent treatment of permanent deacons as a 'proper and permanent rank of the hierarchy' comparable to the treatment given presbyters and bishops in the code; rather, they are treated as exceptions to the norms for presbyters."[6] He expressed hope in his essay that future revisions to the Code of Canon Law would develop such a systematic and coherent legal treatment of the diaconate. Of course, law follows and applies theology. A systematic and coherent theology of the diaconate will be necessary before we can achieve Father Provost's vision.

One problem in describing the specific sacramental identity of the deacon arises from the fact that the theology of orders has usually been developed in terms of the orders of bishop and presbyter, where ordination confers a clear sacramental empowerment. *Lumen gentium* 29 speaks of deacons being "strengthened by sacramental grace," but does not explicate what this might mean. I believe that the work of theologians has begun to develop more substantive understandings of the diaconate, and that recent official documents indicate a growing appreciation that the diaconate must be treated in its own right. The following timeline of selected official documents since 1976, while certainly not exhaustive, is illustrative of this development. I will address several of these points in more detail below.

In 1976, at the express request of Pope Paul VI, the Congregation for the Doctrine of the Faith published *"Inter Insigniores*: Declaration on the Admission of Women to the Ministerial Priesthood." After outlining the teachings of John XXIII and Paul VI on the value of the increasing role of women in the contemporary Church, the Congregation stated that the Church did not have the authority to ordain women to the "ministerial priesthood." Rather pointedly, however, the text goes on to say that "[t]he Catholic Church has never felt that priestly or episcopal ordination can be validly conferred on women." Throughout the remainder of the text, the Congregation repeatedly made specific mention of the priestly order, or the priestly and episcopal orders. In the midst of such specificity and care, it becomes particularly noteworthy that the diaconal order is never once mentioned in the document as being part of the question being addressed.

Additional key documents along the timeline are summarized here:

1. In 1992, the topic of the diaconate was assigned by Cardinal Ratzinger to the International Theological Commission (ITC) as part of its 1992 to 1997 agenda. Deliberations began and were assigned to a subcommission "to analyze some ecclesiological questions."[7]
2. In 1992, the first edition of the *Catechism of the Catholic Church* was released (in French) and included several passages on the diaconate.
3. In 1994, *Ordinatio Sacerdotalis* on the restriction of presbyteral ordination to men alone was promulgated by John Paul II.

4. In 1995, Cardinal Ratzinger's *Responsum ad dubium* concerning *Ordinatio Sacerdotalis* was published.

5. In 1995, the Congregation of the Clergy and the Congregation for Catholic Education published two documents on the presbyterate (one on priestly formation and the other on priestly ministry and life); these two dicasteries immediately announced that two similar documents on the diaconate were in preparation.

6. In 1995, a *plenarium* was held in Rome of the cardinal members of both dicasteries to review the drafts of these documents on the diaconate. Reportedly the question of the possibility of ordaining women as deacons was raised but not resolved, presumably because the ITC had yet to finish its work on the diaconate.

7. [In 1995, the Canon Law Society of America released a study on the canonical implications of the ordination of women to the diaconate. Although the work was not from a Vatican entity, which is why this is bracketed, it is good to note it. The study had been in preparation since 1992. We shall examine the findings below.]

8. In 1997, the topic of the diaconate was reassigned to the ITC for its next five-year commission, because the prior subcommission had been unable to complete a suitable text.

9. In 1997, the pope promulgated the Latin *editio typica* of the *Catechism of the Catholic Church*, which included more than one hundred changes to the original text. One of these changes was significant with regard to the diaconate and will be discussed further below.

10. In 1997, the aforementioned multidicasterial "Instruction on Certain Questions Regarding the Collaboration of the Non-Ordained Faithful in the Sacred Ministry of the Priest" was promulgated.[8] As we shall see, the language involved in this document demonstrates an ongoing lack of theological clarity present in many such texts vis-à-vis the diaconate.

11. In 1998, the Congregation for Clergy and the Congregation for Catholic Education jointly promulgated the *Basic Norms for the Formation of Permanent Deacons* and the *Directory for the Ministry and Life of Permanent Deacons*. No mention was made in either document about the possibility of ordaining women, again presumably because the ITC was still working on the question and had not yet made its recommendations.

12. In 2002, the ITC completed its report and presented it to Cardinal Ratzinger, who authorized its publication.[9]

13. In 2009, Pope Benedict XVI released *motu proprio* the apostolic letter *Omnium in mentem* "on several amendments to the Code of Canon Law." One of these amendments continued the clarification of the canonical standing of the deacon.

14. In 2010, the Congregation for the Doctrine of the Faith promulgated "Norms on *Graviora Delicta*" (*Normae de Gravioribus Delictis*); the "attempted ordination" of women is included as a "more serious delict."

We begin with the *Catechism of the Catholic Church*. The two editions of the *Catechism* manifest an interesting development. In the original text, which was in French, it was said in general about all the ordained (that is, bishops, deacons, and presbyters) that, from Christ, "they receive the mission and faculty ('sacred power') to act in the person of Christ the Head."[10] But in the subsequent Latin *editio typica* a distinction is introduced as a revision to this paragraph:

> From Him [Christ], bishops and priests receive the mission and faculty ("sacred power") to act in the person of Christ the Head, while deacons receive the strength to serve the People of God through the ministry of Worship, Word and Charity in communion with the bishop and his presbyterate.[11]

In this second edition, "sacred power" is communicated by the sacrament of orders only to bishops and presbyters, while deacons receive an unspecified "strength" to serve.

The events surrounding the promulgation of *Ordinatio Sacerdotalis* are also illustrative. In 1994 Pope John Paul II released his apostolic letter *Ordinatio Sacerdotalis* ("On Reserving Priestly Ordination to Men Alone"), addressed to the bishops of the Catholic Church. The pope concludes his letter by writing:

> Although the teaching that priestly ordination is to be reserved to men alone has been preserved by the constant and universal Tradition of the Church and firmly taught by the Magisterium in its more recent documents, at the present time in some places it is nonetheless considered still open to debate, or the Church's judgment that women are not to be admitted to ordination is considered to have a merely disciplinary force. Wherefore, in order that all doubt may be removed regarding a

matter of great importance, a matter which pertains to the Church's divine constitution itself, in
virtue of my ministry of confirming the brethren
(cf. Lk 22:32), I declare that the Church has no
authority whatsoever to confer priestly ordination
on women and that this judgment is to be definitively held by all the Church's faithful.[12]

Immediately questions were raised about the magisterial weight of the document, especially since the term *definitively* was not a term common in papal documents; for
example, then, was it to be understood as the equivalent of
*infallibly*? The following year, a formal question (*dubium*)
was submitted to Cardinal Ratzinger at the Congregation for
the Doctrine of the Faith:

Dubium: Whether the teaching that the Church
has no authority whatsoever to confer priestly
ordination on women, which is presented in the
Apostolic Letter *Ordinatio Sacerdotalis* to be held
definitively, is to be understood as belonging to
the deposit of faith....

[And in his affirmative response, Cardinal
Ratzinger wrote:] This teaching requires definitive assent, since, founded on the written Word of
God, and from the beginning constantly preserved
and applied in the Tradition of the Church, it has
been set forth infallibly by the ordinary and universal Magisterium (cf. *Lumen gentium*, 25).[13]

In short, according to the response, the position taken in
*Ordinatio Sacerdotalis* is definitive teaching, not under the
rubric of an exercise of papal infallibility, but because the

entire magisterium of the Church has so determined. Theologians and canonists across the theological spectrum continue to explore the ramifications of this teaching and its reception.

As interesting as all of this is, however, we must attend to something even more pertinent to our particular topic: *this entire teaching concerns the priesthood, not the diaconate*. The pope never referred explicitly to the diaconate, nor used more inclusive terms such as *clergy* (which would include bishops, presbyters, *and* deacons). Therefore, the specific question arises: Does the teaching of *Ordinatio Sacerdotalis*—"On Reserving Priestly Ordination to Men Alone"—apply to the diaconate as well as to the priesthood, specifically, the presbyterate?

It seems clear from the other actions taken by the Holy See that it does not. As noted in the timeline, between 1992 and 2002, the subject of the diaconate was given by Cardinal Ratzinger to the International Theological Commission as part of their successive agendas. As noted in the timeline, the first five-year commission was unable to complete a suitable text by the end of its term. Notice that this work brackets the developments of the *Catechism*, as well as the issues surrounding *Ordinatio Sacerdotalis*. I would also point out the development of two groups of documents, one on the presbyterate (1995) and the other on the diaconate (1998). Still another group of documents reveal a less-well-defined treatment of the clergy in general. While it would be wrong to ascribe an intentional connection between these events, I believe that it illustrates a significant point.

Specifically, the events suggest that the Holy See was proceeding on three parallel courses with regard to ordained ministries. There is one set of documents devoted specifically to the presbyterate, for example, *Ordinatio Sacerdotalis*.

Another set of documents is devoted specifically to the diaconate, for example, *Directory for the Ministry and Life of Deacons*. In these two sets of documents, the treatment of presbyters and the treatment of deacons are carefully and intentionally distinct. Then there is a third set of documents, such as the multidicasterial "Instruction" referenced above, in which the language is not clearly distinguished at all, with terms such as *ordination* and *clergy* (which would apply to all bishops, presbyters, and deacons) used rather indiscriminately. The intention, perhaps, was to make a statement about the presbyterate; however, by using the more general, more inclusive terms, it would seem that the statement was being made about the diaconate as well. This added to the confusion of the time.

The interdicasterial "Instruction on Certain Questions Regarding the Collaboration of the Non-Ordained Faithful in the Sacred Ministry of Priest" is quite inconsistent in its treatment of deacons. In several passages, deacons and their functions are clearly included in the category of "sacred ministers"; in others, comments appear to be restricted to those in sacerdotal orders. Consider just one passage as an example:

> The characteristics which differentiate the ministerial priesthood of Bishops and Priests from the common priesthood of the faithful...may be summarized in the following fashion:
>
> a) the ministerial priesthood is rooted in the Apostolic Succession, and vested with potestas sacra consisting of the faculty and the responsibility of acting in the person of Christ the Head and the Shepherd;
>
> b) it is a priesthood which renders its sacred ministers servants of Christ and of the Church by

means of authoritative proclamation of the Word of God, the administration of the sacraments and the pastoral direction of the faithful....

The ordained ministry, therefore, is established on the foundation of the Apostles for the upbuilding of the Church: "and is completely at the service of the Church." "Intrinsically linked to the sacramental nature of ecclesial ministry is its character of service. Entirely dependent on Christ who gives mission and authority, ministers are truly 'servants of Christ' (*Rom* 1, 1) in the image of him who freely took for us 'the form of a slave' (*Phil* 2,7). Because the word and grace of which they are ministers are not their own, but are given to them by Christ for the sake of others, they must freely become the slaves of all."[14]

While this passage refers specifically to the ministerial priesthood of bishops and priests, it also seems applicable to deacons. Sacred ministers are referred to as "servants" of God and the Church, fulfilling functions of Word, sacrament, and "pastoral direction": functions applicable in various ways to deacons. In the final paragraph, sacred ministry is described through reference to the kenotic hymn of Philippians 2.[15]

Surely no other reference could be more applicable to the ministry of deacons. Paul, writing from prison, is exhorting the Philippians to be "of the same mind, having the same love, being in full accord."[16] He tells them to "do nothing from selfish ambition or conceit, but in humility regard others as better than yourselves. Let each of you look not to your own interests, but to the interests of others."[17] It is here that Paul does an interesting thing: after writing that the Philippians should have the same attitude as Christ, he inserts in his letter the lyrics of an early Christian hymn which states that Christ, "though he was in the form of God, did not regard equality with God something to be grasped. Rather he emptied himself, taking on the form of a slave."[18]

Turning back now to the third category of official documents, in which the language about deacons is indistinct, we find the *Catechism of the Catholic Church*. By studying the successive editions of the *Catechism*, however, we can discern the influence of the work being done on the diaconate as the text of the *Catechism* underwent revision and development. In fact, the development of the *Catechism* has now been applied to canon law, as seen in the 2009 apostolic letter *Omnium in mentem*, which revised canon law to reflect the same adjustment that had already been made in the *editio typica* of the *Catechism*.

In short, the diaconate is *not* the presbyterate, and we operate from the premise that the diaconate must be understood and examined in its own right and on its own merits. Those documents that treat the diaconate as distinct from the presbyterate are much more precise; those documents that treat all orders without distinction become far more problematic. Echoing James Provost, we state that theological discourse must continue to assist in this development of distinct terminology with regard to the diaconate. To the specific concern of this book, then, questions of whether or not women may, or should, be ordained as deacons need to be dealt with separately from the ministerial priesthood.

That being said, we again look at the Second Vatican Council to see if we may find specific insights into the hopes and visions of the council fathers as they moved toward the decision to renew a permanent diaconate.

# Vatican II and Its Vision of the Diaconate: Grace in Action

I have written elsewhere and far more extensively about the development of the various proposals considered by the Council, as well as the conciliar discussions and debates leading up to the decision to renew the diaconate.[19] While we do not have the opportunity to review this rich history in detail here, we will sketch the parameters in broad strokes. Furthermore, space does not permit a review of conciliar decisions vis-à-vis the overall role of the laity in ministry, including official ministry. I will focus on the Council's view of the diaconate itself.

The popular misperception persists that somehow the effort to renew the diaconate was driven by bishops from the developing nations. However, there were at least four major influences leading up to the consideration of the question at the Council. First, primarily in Germany in the nineteenth and early twentieth centuries, Catholics and certain Church officials began to discuss the need to expand the role of the deacon, especially in light of Protestant efforts along the same lines, to meet the pastoral needs of German congregations and communities. This includes the rapid development of the German Caritas movement, which became so vital that in 1897 a Caritas organization was mandated for every diocese in Germany. Second, the impact of the Second World War, most especially the experience of German and Polish priests incarcerated at the Dachau concentration camp, was profound. The writings of several priest-survivors after the war gave the existing discussions about a permanent diaconate new urgency and purpose.[20] They also drew the attention of theologians such as Karl Rahner, who began a longstanding contribution to the field of diaconal theology.[21] Third, responding to this growing body of literature, was the growth of the proposal in mission and catechetical fields in the late 1950s, and fourth was the teachings of Pope Pius XII on the sacrament of orders in 1947 and again in 1957. All of this set the stage for the 101 proposals (with some proposals representing whole groups of bishops) concerning the renewal of the diaconate received during the antepreparatory phase of the Council. Far from being an initiative of the bishops from the mission territories alone, the need for a renewed diaconate came most forcefully from bishops from around the world, especially Western and Eastern Europe. At least two of these proposals specifically desired a diaconate open to women.[22]

Sixteen proposals, representing the intervention of seventy-one bishops, offered some idea of the functions that might be assigned to the new permanent deacons who, they hoped, would be forthcoming.[23] In addition to sacramental and liturgical functions, some interesting details included the desire that deacons might serve as ministers of extreme unction (the sacrament of the sick) and thus "bring solace to the faithful in extreme situations."[24] Administration of the Church's temporal goods, long associated with the diaconate, is prominent on the lists of proposed functions, but the single most important functions listed are those of official preaching and teaching.[25] The following table outlines these functions:[26]

| Antepreparatory Proposals for the Functions of Deacons | | |
|---|---|---|
| PROPOSAL | TEXT | SUPPORTING SEES |
| 1 | Deacons should be forty years old, and their doctrine and morals should be investigated. | 2 |
| 2 | Deacons should be forty years old and exemplary catechists. | 1 |

# WOMEN DEACONS: PRESENT POSSIBILITIES

| PROPOSAL | TEXT | SUPPORTING SEES |
|:---:|:---|:---:|
| 3 | The following offices are the deacons': preaching, baptizing, distributing Holy Communion, exposing the Blessed Sacrament for adoration, giving the eucharistic blessing, and taking viaticum to the sick. | 3 |
| 4 | Deacons may be installed, especially in mission areas and where there is a shortage of priests, for the following offices: solemn administration of baptism; valid assistance at marriages; administration of the Holy Eucharist, even as viaticum; proclamation of the Word of God in church; and administration of the goods of the church. | 2 |
| 5 | Deacons should be of mature age; of evident Christian spirit; of sufficient knowledge of dogmatics, morals, scriptures, and liturgy. Their offices may be to catechize, to assist the parish priest in the Eucharist, and to distribute Holy Communion to the faithful, upon the prudent judgment of the parish priest. | 25 |
| 6 | Deacons are bound by the law of residency, under the supervision of the parish priest, and sustained by the faithful or by the curia. | 1 |
| 7 | Deacons may assist at marriages. | 5 |
| 8 | Deacons may be granted the faculty to preside at Solemn Benediction with the Blessed Sacrament. | 3 |
| 9 | The administration of the temporal goods of the church may be transferred by the parish priest to the deacon so that the parish priests may focus on spiritual care. | 1 |
| 10 | Deacons attend to the administration of goods. | 1 |
| 11 | In accordance with canon 938, the deacon may be the extraordinary minister of extreme unction when there are not enough priests or there is an urgent necessity. | 1 |
| 12 | Deacons may confer extreme unction in the absence of priests. | 1 |

| PROPOSAL | TEXT | SUPPORTING SEES |
|---|---|---|
| 13 | Deacons may bring solace to the faithful in extreme situations. | 21 |
| 14 | Deacons may conduct burials. | 2 |
| 15 | The order of the diaconate may be conferred on catechists and assisting laity. | 1 |
| 16 | Deacons may be named as professors of religion. | 1 |

In the preconciliar commissions, discussions on the diaconate highlighted other points. The diaconate was perceived as related to, but distinct from, the presbyterate. For this reason, for example, it was argued that deacons should be of a more mature age (several proposals specified forty as the minimum age for ordination)[27] and that since they were not priests, these deacons could be married. Although the question of opening the diaconate to married men was heatedly debated during the Council, the vast majority of bishops favored the idea. Ultimately, the voting on celibacy was 1,598 in favor of ordaining married men and 629 against.[28]

Forty-five bishops, speaking on behalf of 795 fathers, spoke in favor of a permanent diaconate; twenty-five speakers, representing only eighty-two fathers, spoke against the idea. The debate was held from October 4 to 16, 1963.[29]

The first speaker in favor of a renewed diaconate was Cardinal Julius Döpfner of the Archdiocese of Munich-Freising.[30] This young cardinal archbishop, only forty-nine when the Council began in 1962, had extensive pastoral experience, starting in 1939 when he was ordained a priest of the Diocese of Würzburg. At age thirty-five he became the bishop of Würzburg. He would then serve as bishop of Berlin before becoming the archbishop of Munich-Freising in 1961. Rising at the Council to speak, Döpfner strongly urged acceptance of the proposal to renew the diaconate. He supported the inclusion of the diaconate in a dogmatic document[31] because the orders of the hierarchy of the Church was a dogmatic issue, part of the divine law, and therefore an essential part of the nature of the Church. He pointed out that the diaconate, ever since Trent, had been seen as part of the sacramental priesthood. Döpfner pointed to the fact that many persons, many of them married, were already serving the Church in diaconal roles. In his intervention, he asked, "Why should these people be denied the grace of the sacrament?"[32] He affirmed the value of clerical celibacy, but he also declared that celibacy should not become an obstacle for the evolution of beneficial ways to serve that may be necessary in our time.

Following the interventions of several more supporters of a renewed diaconate, Cardinal Leo-Josef Suenens of Malines-Brussels presented what is arguably the strongest and most coherent argument for the diaconate evident in the documents.[33] Another young, brilliant, and pastorally experienced leader, Suenens had been ordained a priest for the Archdiocese of Malines-Brussels at age twenty-three. In 1940, after serving as the vice rector of the University of Louvain, he became acting rector when the Nazis arrested the incumbent. He served with great courage and integrity throughout the war, and was eventually placed on a Nazi execution list. He was saved by the Allied liberation of Belgium in 1944. After the war, he became bishop and eventually a cardinal shortly before the Council opened. A close and trusted collaborator of Pope John XXIII, Suenens was an important influence on the Council and its work.

Before the Council began, Suenens had already included a renewed diaconate as part of his own hopes for the Council. During the antepreparatory phase, Suenens indicated his support in his antepreparatory *votum* of November 10,

1959.[34] First alluding to a 1957 address by Pius XII,[35] in which the pope had observed that the question of restoring the diaconate was not yet ripe but was worthy of continued attention, Suenens wrote that the Council would provide a most appropriate opportunity to highlight this question, and that a diaconate distinct and separate from the priesthood, a state to which married men might also be admitted, would be part of a movement of overall renewal in the Church. He also wrote that the diaconate was one of several ministries consistently and traditionally recognized in the life of the Church. He continued by pointing out that the Church has a command from the Lord to proclaim the Gospel to all peoples and to baptize all nations.

Such a task would be impossible without the coming together of all the faithful, especially those whose lives were devoted to the mission of evangelization. The deacon was presented as a minister of this evangelization who could be assigned to serve in different ways, depending upon the pastoral needs of the area in which he served, including the proclamation of the Gospels, catechesis, and other areas for the work of redemption. Cardinal Suenens would write later, "Undoubtedly, this decision [to renew the permanent diaconate] was made for pastoral reasons, but these were not the only factors operative. The restoration of a Permanent Diaconate finds its fundamental clarification and justification in the sacramental character of the diaconate itself."[36] During the conciliar debate, it would be Suenens himself who attempted to articulate this "sacramental character of the diaconate."

Suenens began by outlining the theological principles upon which the diaconate is based. Citing the authority of Scripture, the apostolic fathers, constant tradition, and the liturgical books of East and West, he spoke of the many charisms evident throughout the Church, distinct from the priesthood, which were established to provide direct assistance to the bishop in the care of the poor and the nurturing of the community. He wrote that simply saying such tasks can be given to laypersons does not mean that the diaconate is not needed. These tasks should only be given to persons (whether ordained or not) who have the necessary graces. The Church has the right to the benefit of all the graces given to it by God, including the graces of the diaconate.[37]

Suenens urged the council fathers not to make a universal decision for or against the diaconate. Rather, they should decide if there was any area or situation that might benefit from it, and then phrase the Council's decision in such a manner as to enable it to take effect in those regions where local bishops deemed it appropriate. In other words, the Council should not close off universally any means by which the grace of God might flow into the Church. Therefore (quoting from the draft text of *Lumen gentium*), "where episcopal conferences judge the restoration of a permanent diaconate opportune, they should be free to introduce it."[38]

The conciliar debates led to a final vote in overwhelming support of a renewed diaconate, addressed directly in #29 of *Lumen gentium*. However, the vision of the bishops regarding a renewed diaconate is evident in other ways as well. While *LG* 29 is the principle conciliar text on the diaconate, it is not the only one. The restoration of a permanent diaconate, mandated for the Western Church, was strongly encouraged for the Eastern Catholic Churches.[39] The diaconate is referred to as well in the constitutions *Sacrosanctum Concilium* (#35) and *Dei Verbum* (#25). Particularly interesting is the insight offered in #16 of the decree *Ad gentes divinitus* (on the "Missionary Activity of the Church"), which echoes Suenens' teaching on the grace of the sacrament:

Where episcopal conferences deem it opportune, the order of the diaconate should be restored as a permanent state of life according to the norms of the Constitution *"De Ecclesia."* For there are men who actually carry out the functions of the deacon's office, either preaching the word of God as catechists, or presiding over scattered Christian communities in the name of the pastor and the bishop, or practicing charity in social or relief work. It is only right to strengthen them by the imposition of hands which has come down from the Apostles, and to bind them more closely to the altar, that they may carry out their ministry more effectively because of the sacramental grace of the diaconate.[40]

The Council's teaching about the diaconate was grounded in the Church's understanding of grace as God's gift to the entire people of God. Within this ecclesial context, deacons were said to be "strengthened by sacramental grace" (*LG* 29) and that it was "only right" to strengthen persons who were already exercising diaconal functions with the grace of ordination in order "to bind them more closely to the altar" and so that they might perform more effectively the functions they were already performing (*AG* 16). These references summarized the interventions of Suenens and other council fathers during the debates on the diaconate.

The following points may be taken from this quick review of the Council's work:

1. The diaconate is distinct from the presbyterate. While there was some discussion that deacons could be helpful in areas with a shortage of presbyters, the

far more substantive rationale for restoring the permanent diaconate was that, following the horrors of war and violence, the Church needed a new form of ordained ministry, one that modeled Christ the Servant. While the diaconate would remain a transitional order for those preparing for the presbyterate, the new "norm" became and remains a diaconate exercised as its own permanent state of life; the diaconate no longer finds its sacramental end in the presbyterate. This diaconal state of life would be expressed in ways distinct from the presbyterate as well. The most obvious differences, for example, would include:

    a. deacons might be married;

    b. deacons are expected to live and minister "in the world";

    c. the diaconate is a flexible response by the Church made at the discretion of local conferences of bishops.

2. The Church should benefit from all of the graces given by God, and the diaconate has been a charism of and for the Church throughout Christian history.

3. Those who exercise diaconal ministries should receive the sacramental grace of the sacrament.

4. The renewed diaconate is not simply a restoration of the ancient diaconate. It is a new expression of this ministry in the Church. This means that appeals to history, while helpful, are not prescriptive or delimiting.

5. The renewal of a permanent diaconate took place, literally and theologically, within the renewal of the episcopacy itself. Given the biblical and patristic association of the deacon with the bishop, this is par-

ticularly appropriate. The diaconate needs to be understood within this context. The deacon and bishop have a unique relationship. While one often hears of the unique relationship that exists between presbyters and their bishop, a similar relationship exists between deacons and their bishop.

6. The Church's cadre of "servants"—the diaconate— finds its place and sacramental significance within the larger context of a diaconal Church.

This last point is perhaps the most profound gift of the Council to the Church. Throughout the years of the Council, the bishops gained a new sense of their own mission and the very nature of the Church in the modern world. When Pope Paul VI concluded the Council, he reminded the bishops that "the teaching of the Council is channeled in one direction, the service of humankind, of every condition, in every weakness and need. The Church has declared herself a servant of humanity....The idea of service has been central."[41]

Paul VI referred to the diaconate as "the driving force" for the Church's own *diaconia*, and successive popes have echoed the same theme: John Paul II taught that "the service of the deacon is the Church's service sacramentalized.... [Deacons] are meant to be living signs of the servanthood of Christ's Church";[42] Benedict XVI developed the thought even further. In *Deus Caritas Est*, he wrote:

A decisive step in the difficult search for ways of putting this fundamental ecclesial principle into practice is illustrated in the choice of the seven, which marked the origin of the diaconal office (cf. Acts 6:5–6)....The social service which they were meant to provide was absolutely concrete, yet at the same time it was also a spiritual service; theirs was a truly spiritual office which carried out an essential responsibility of the Church, namely a well-ordered love of neighbor. With the formation of this group of seven, "*diaconia*"—the ministry of charity exercised in a communitarian, orderly way—became part of the fundamental structure of the Church.[43]

Just as we are all part of a "royal priesthood" (1 Pet 2:9), we are all part of a servant Church. Our ordained priests (bishops and presbyters) and ordained deacons serve as the "driving force" and sacramental signs to the identity into which all participate through initiation.

## WOMEN AS DEACONS IN THE CONTEMPORARY CHURCH

So we arrive at the central question of this essay. Shall women once again be ordained deacons in the Catholic Church?

Mention has been made several times of the ten years of work that two successive quinquennia of the International Theological Commission have devoted to the subject of the diaconate. Of particular interest is the text released by the Commission in 2002. "From the point of view of its theological meaning and its ecclesial role the ministry of the diaconate presents a challenge to the Church's awareness and practice, particularly through the questions that it still raises today."[44] The Commission points out that there is one sacrament of orders; conversely, it acknowledges the difference in this one sacrament between the sacerdotal orders of bishop and presbyter on the one hand, and the diaconal order on the other. This distinction is made within the ITC text as well as in the *Catechism of the Catholic Church* and, most recently, in canon law. And herein lies the challenge: If one focuses on the unicity of orders, then one could argue that an inability to ordain a person to one order would make ordination to any order impossible. If the focus is on the diversity within order, one might argue that we risk losing the unity of the sacrament as participations in the one priesthood of Christ.

Given the developments outlined in the first part of this essay, I submit that since the early 1990s there has been a growing sophistication in articulating the very real distinctions present within the one sacrament of orders. The changes made in the *Catechism*, and more recently the refinements made in canon law, suggest an attempt to balance this diversity-in-unity. As we have noted repeatedly, deacons are not priests. With two identified modalities of participation in the one sacrament, each modality must be assessed in its own right.

I believe that this appreciative attitude toward this dual modality is present not only in papal and curial documents, but in the entire approach of the Second Vatican Council regarding the diaconate. Even though the permanent diaconate was only a dream at the Council, the fathers seemed to realize that this renewed ministry was going to need to be developed in new, diverse ways if the diaconate was to actualize its potential. This led them, for example, to open up the diaconate to married as well as celibate men, while retaining the general requirement of celibacy for the Latin presbyterate. While deacons would participate in the threefold *munus—docendi, sanctificandi*, and *regendi—*of all the ordained, the specifics of how this participation was to be carried out would be distinctive from the priesthood, and the council fathers knew that. In fact, it was precisely to extend the reach of the Church into areas not being served adequately that underscored the need for a permanent diaconate in the first place. Pope John Paul II once recalled that "a deeply felt need in the decision to reestablish the diaconate was and is that of a greater and more direct presence of Church ministers in the various spheres such as family, work, school, etc., in addition to existing pastoral structures."[45]

Immediately after outlining the unicity and diversity of orders, the International Theological Commission concluded its text by addressing our question: "It pertains to the ministry of discernment which the Lord established in his Church to pronounce authoritatively on this question."[46] In short, the Commission chose not to answer the question. Although there is a tendency in the text to stress the unicity of orders, the members of the Commission refused to rule out the possibility of women being ordained as deacons; they do not, for example, link the diaconate to the teaching of *Ordinatio Sacerdotalis*. Instead, the ITC points the way ahead for the Church to render a separate authoritative decision on the diaconate, implying that the decision might be different from decisions made regarding the presbyterate.

In 1995, the Canon Law Society of America released a study entitled "The Canonical Implications of Ordaining Women to the Permanent Diaconate."[47] The study asks:

Today, is diaconal ordination of women necessary or at least useful for promoting the mission of evangelization and pastoral care which Christ entrusted to the Church to carry out in the world, particularly in the United States? Does the breadth and diversity of the Church's communion embrace the possibility of ordination of women to the permanent diaconate in at least some local areas of the communion, much as ordination of men to the permanent diaconate has become an option in some local areas of the Church without it being necessarily embraced by all areas of the Church?[48]

The study concluded that "the supreme authority of the Church is competent to decide to ordain women to the permanent diaconate."[49] On a practical level:

The amount of adjustments in law which would be required to open the permanent diaconate to women are within the authority of the Church to make, and are relatively few in number. The practical effect, however, would be to open up ordained ministry as permanent deacons to women, enabling them to receive all seven sacraments, and making them capable of assuming offices which entail the exercise of the diaconal order and of ecclesiastical jurisdiction, which are now closed to women because they are closed to lay persons.[50]

In the context of the material examined in this essay, these observations seem particularly apt. Just as the council fathers at the Second Vatican Council, under the leadership of bishops such as Suenens and Döpfner, challenged the imagination of their brothers to the possibility of an expanded and renewed diaconate based on the needs of the Church and the multiple gifts of the Holy Spirit, so too would the ordination of women as deacons continue this process. In all of the pertinent official literature, nothing substantive impedes this possibility.

## CONCLUSIONS

The sacrament of orders has always been characterized by its great sacramental diversity and flexibility. To understand what I mean by "sacramental diversity," consider the following: Throughout the period of the *cursus honorum* that existed until 1972, the Latin system of orders contained a liturgical rite that was not in itself an ordination (first tonsure), ordinations that were not sacramental (the four minor orders and the major order of subdiaconate), a major order that was sacramental but not priestly (the diaconate), and a third major order that was sacramental and priestly (the presbyterate). So the notion of diversity of expression within the one sacrament of orders is not a new or radical idea. In the older system of the *cursus honorum*, of course, what little "theology of the diaconate" existed merely spoke of the deacon as participating in a limited way in the priesthood, and the deacon, sacramentally and canonically, would be expected eventually to move into the priesthood.

With the paradigm shift wrought by the Second Vatican Council, and the reintroduction of a permanent diaconate, this theology had to change of necessity. No longer understood as a lesser participation in the priesthood, the diaconate emerges as a "proper and stable" order. An appropriate sacramental diversity again exists within the sacrament of orders. No longer is the lens of the ministerial priesthood the only way to understand the nature of ordained ministry. What we learn from recent history is that each order, while certainly related and grounded in Christ, has its own sacramental identity. There is one sacrament, with two distinct modes of participation in that sacrament. One mode is that of the ministerial priesthood consisting of the order of bishops and the order of presbyters; the second modality is that of the order of deacons. Within the modality of the diaconate, the possibility that women can and should be ordained as deacons in the contemporary Church is theologically and canonically justifiable.

Just as the older system gave way to the changing needs of the Church, the current system will need to be just as flexible as we continue to "read the signs of the times in light of the Gospel." Just as the Second Vatican Council could begin the process of making certain features of the diaconate distinct from the priesthood (namely, by opening ordination to married men), it seems clear that the Church can do the same now by ordaining women as deacons.

Deacons, according to papal teaching, are to animate and sacramentalize the Church's own service; women have always been critically important ministers of *diakonia*, and the ministry and effectiveness of the deacon will be enriched beyond measure by the ordination of women into the order of deacons. Two voices from the Second Vatican Council continue to inspire and challenge us. Cardinal Suenens, as we have seen, repeatedly stressed that the Church is entitled to all of the graces the Holy Spirit provides, and one of those graces is the diaconate: Why should the Church be denied the gift of women as well as men serving as deacons?

As we saw, Cardinal Döpfner recognized that many people, even some ineligible for ordination, were already serving the Church in diaconal roles. In his intervention, he asked, "Why should these people be denied the grace of the sacrament?"[51] We now apply his question to the countless women who are selflessly serving in servant roles throughout the world. Cardinal Döpfner's question echoes through the years: "Why should these people be denied the grace of the sacrament?"

# WOMEN DEACONS: FUTURE

## Phyllis Zagano

What can be said of the future of women deacons in the Catholic Church?

Professor Macy's discussion of the history of women ordained to the diaconate pinpoints the way in which women were eliminated from any consideration for the sacrament of orders. Despite their long history of service, the concurrent marginalization of women in ministry, importation of ancient taboos regarding women's bodies, and emerging theology of ordination conjoined to argue that even if women were to be ordained, nothing would happen—it wouldn't "take." This outlook, however, appeared and was codified only in the Middle Ages, after the diaconate as a separate and distinct order had generally died out. So, by the time Gratian of Bologna is arguing against women as deacons, he is mostly arguing against women as deacons who would be considered on the road to priesthood. The priesthood presented the problem, not the diaconate.

Professor Ditewig, meanwhile, presents the modern understanding of the diaconate. In tracing the contemporary history of the restoration of the diaconate, he underscores the fact that the clear distinction between the priesthood and the diaconate does not disturb the unicity of orders; rather, it enhances the unicity and allows a rejuvenated understanding of the possibilities for including women in the order of deacon.

Do the past and present predict a future for women as deacons in the Catholic Church? History, while not normative one way or the other, is certainly informative. Contemporary calls for the restoration of women to the diaconate in the Catholic Church, from both the hierarchy and the people of God, evidence the deep interest and need for the Church to restore its tradition. However, for the tradition of women deacons to be genuinely carried forth, it must be continued as an ordained ministry.

## WHAT DIFFERENCE WOULD ORDINATION MAKE?

Within the current discussion about the restoration of women to the ordained diaconate arises the comment that there is nothing an ordained deacon can do that a woman cannot do—implying, it would seem, that ordination is a useless adjunct to diaconal service. The comment was voiced publicly by Cardinal Walter Kasper, former president of the Pontifical Council for Promoting Christian Unity and, not incidentally, cardinal deacon of the Roman Church Ognissanti ("All Saints") in Via Appia Nuova.

In 2005, Kasper told a reporter in New York that women are already doing what they would be able to do if they were ordained as deacons.[1] He said this despite his paper affirming the value of the restored diaconate, delivered at the 1997 International Diaconate Center Study Conference in Brixen, Italy. There Kasper defended the ordained diaconate, noting at the outset that "merely to claim that the Diaconate continues to be a fundamental and necessary ministry in our Church can lead to some heated debates. For a long time now the Diaconate has not necessarily been firmly established in all local churches."[2]

Kasper reflects an interesting stance: the diaconate is important and women are welcome to do its work, but women may not share in the grace of the charism of the order. The fathers of the Second Vatican Council apparently agree that the diaconate is important, as the history of their interventions and determinations proves. Further, the predominance of historical evidence points to many bishops (and popes) throughout history who included women in the order of deacon, women who ministered in the traditionally understood social-service ministries of the diaconate, as well as women who performed liturgical ministries.

So, if women once were deacons, and the diaconate is necessary to the contemporary Church (as it has been reestablished and reinvigorated as a permanent order of ministry), what restricts women from reentering it?

## STATEMENTS FROM ROME

Cardinal Kasper admitted in 2005 that the question of ordaining women as deacons is "not settled."[3] Indeed, it is not. While the law forbids the ordination of women as deacons, no contemporary doctrine on the matter has been defined.

In 2001, three curial offices—the Congregation for the Doctrine of the Faith, the Congregation for Divine Worship and the Discipline of the Sacraments, and the Congregation for Clergy—issued a "notification" on the diaconal ordination of women that appears to have been directed at the bishops of Germany, who apparently wanted to prepare women for ordained diaconal ministry. The notification stated that "it is not licit to enact initiatives which, in some

way, aim to prepare [women] candidates for diaconal ordination."[4] In essence, the four-paragraph notification stated
that women should not be prepared for the diaconate
because church law disallows their ordination. A notification
is a low-level document that restates a policy, but makes no
comment or determination about doctrine.

The highest-level contemporary official statement
addressing theological questions surrounding women deacons is the 2002 report of the International Theological
Commission (ITC) entitled *Le Diaconat: Évolution et perspectives* and officially published only in French. While the ITC
questions the historical record, it expressly leaves open the
possibility of women deacons, determining that the question
of ordaining women as deacons is "up to the magisterium."
That is, the document stated officially what Cardinal Kasper
would say later: the matter is not settled.

In large part, the ITC document does not address the
needs of the Church for diaconal ministry by women, but
rather looks to history to provide substance for its wish to
deny any evidence of the sacramental ordination of women
as deacons. That is, the ITC document addresses history, but
does not interpret the historical evidence of women deacons
in the most positive light. The Commission wrote:

> Regarding the ordination of women to the diac-
> onate, it should be noted that two important
> points emerge from what has been set forth here:
> 1) the deaconesses mentioned in the ancient tra-
> dition of the Church—as suggested by their rite
> of institution and the functions they exercised—
> are not purely and simply the same as deacons;
> 2) the unity of the sacrament of order, in the clear
> distinction between the ministries of the bishop

and the priest on the one hand and the ministry of the deacon on the other, is strongly underscored by ecclesial tradition, above all in the doctrine of Vatican Council II and the postconciliar teaching of the Magisterium. In the light of these elements, supported by the evidence of the present historical-theological research, it will be up to the ministry of discernment, which the Lord has established in his Church, to speak authoritatively on this question.[5]

Hence, the International Theological Commission of the Congregation of the Doctrine of the Faith, under the presidency of Cardinal Joseph Ratzinger, concluded in 2002 that (1) the history of deaconesses does not support a historical argument for women deacons, and (2) the sacrament of orders clearly distinguishes between the ministries of the bishop and priest and those of the deacon.

As Professor Macy has demonstrated, there is substantial historical evidence regarding women deacons, the ceremonials attached to their creation, and their roles and functions.

As Professor Ditewig has demonstrated, the evolving theology of the diaconate distinguishes bishop and priest from deacon in ways that apparently allow for return to the earlier tradition of women deacons.

In fact, the Commission's real conclusion is that "it is up to the ministry of discernment, which the Lord has established in his Church, to speak authoritatively" and make the decision on women deacons. How long that determination will take is unclear. From the historical perspective, both the ordinary magisterium (for example, Pope Benedict VIII in his letter to the bishop of Porto)[6] and the extraordinary magisterium (the Councils of Nicaea and Chalcedon) have already made positive determinations about the ordination of women to the diaconate.[7]

But, how is the combined ordinary and extraordinary magisterium of history transported to the present? Some take the position that a diocesan bishop already has the juridical authority and sacramental power to ordain a woman to the diaconate for service in his diocese, and that the decision should be his in concert with his episcopal conference. Most take the position that despite papal letters and conciliar statements, diocesan bishops do not have such juridical authority and sacramental power (even prior to the newest rulings of the Congregation for the Doctrine of the Faith regarding any ordination of a woman—priestly or diaconal).[8] Even if at some point future bishops may in concert with Rome ordain women as deacons, the freedom to accept or reject including women in the diaconate would ultimately rest with the diocesan bishop. That is, if a bishop determined that he needed women deacons, he would be able to ordain them within his diocese. Conversely, if a bishop determined that he did not need women deacons, he could refuse them within his diocese.[9]

The question of magisterial determination is crucial. At present, there is no Church doctrine against ordaining women to the diaconate. There are, however, expanded delineations of Canon 1024 stating that only males are validly ordained, as well as administrative objections from curial offices. Theoretically, at least, a bishop might request a derogation from the law. But, what bishop would formally request a derogation without the whole Church voicing its need and agreeing to the restoration of the older practice?

The International Theological Commission looks toward the "ministry of discernment" in the Church to answer the question. What comprises the contemporary discernment necessary for the Church to return to its older tradition? Several Latin bishops have broached the question with the pope in *ad limina* visits, and many have called publicly for women deacons. As Professor Ditewig pointed out, during the Second Vatican Council both Peruvian Bishop León Bonaventura de Uriarte Bengoa, OFM (1891–1970), and Bishop Giuseppe Ruotolo (1898–1970) of Ugento, Italy, suggested that women be included in the restored order of deacon.[10] More recently, several others, including the late Basil Cardinal Hume[11] and Cardinal Carlo Maria Martini, called for women deacons.[12] Other bishops have asked for women deacons in *ad limina* meetings.[13] Since other Christian Churches recognized by the Holy See as having valid sacraments and orders have already decided positively on ordaining women to the diaconate (for example, the Orthodox Church of Greece and the Armenian Apostolic Church),[14] one can ask whether their practice might influence the magisterium. For example, Bartholomew, Ecumenical Patriarch of Constantinople, has affirmed the possibility of returning to this "ancient tradition of the Church."[15]

## OBJECTIONS TO ORDAINING WOMEN

It is important to recall that the stated objections to women priests do not apply to women deacons: The seven usually considered the first deacons were put forth by the Church and accepted by the apostles (Acts 6:1–6). They served "not the priesthood, but the ministry." In fact, the only person in Scripture to hold the actual title "deacon" is Phoebe, deacon (not deaconess) of the church at Cenchreae (Rom 16:1).

In 2009, the distinction between priest and deacon was again stipulated. Following the 1997 *Catechism of the Catholic Church*, Pope Benedict XVI's *motu proprio Omnium in Mentem* clarified canon law regarding the distinction: priests are ordained to act in the person of Christ, the head of the Church; deacons are ordained to serve the people of God in and through the Word, the liturgy, and charity. In addition, Benedict XVI has several times called directly for including women in formal governance and ministry. If we subscribe to the most formal terminology, ordaining women as deacons is the way they can be so included. That is, "governance" and "ministry" in the hierarchical Church can only be rendered by the ordained. If the pope intends women to be included—formally—in governance and ministry, he can do so by returning to the tradition of women deacons.[16]

The problem for most naysayers, apparently including Kasper, is not the question of deacons. It may not even be the question of women deacons. Rather, it is the question of *ordained* women deacons.

Ordained women deacons raise two distinct problems. First, it would appear at first glance that if you can ordain a woman a deacon, you can then ordain her a priest or bishop. Even if that objection is overcome, there is a second problem: because the ordinary means of entering the clerical state is by ordination to the diaconate, ordaining women as deacons would create a cadre of female clerics. So the problem is immediately twofold: (1) ordained women deacons portend women priests; (2) ordained women are clerics.

While the former—women deacons portend women priests—is a fear often voiced, it is in fact a red herring, possibly presented to deter investigation of the latter. That is, either the Church teaches and agrees that women cannot be ordained priests and bishops, or it does not. If it does not agree to its own teaching, a teaching argued by many to be included in the magisterium to the point of near infallibility (recall Cardinal Ratzinger's *Responsum ad dubium*), then indeed women ordained to the diaconate might presumably "advance" to the priesthood and the episcopacy.[17] But the Church teaches that women cannot be ordained as priests or bishops; it also teaches that there is a distinct order of the diaconate. Therefore, if a woman cannot be ordained as priest or bishop, then a woman ordained to the "permanent" diaconate would be just that—a permanent deacon.

There are other hurdles for women prior to diaconal ordination. A candidate must first have been formally installed as both lector and acolyte, which is currently impossible, although the 2008 Synod of Bishops on the Word of God recommended opening the formal ministry of lector to women.[18] Once ordained, a deacon enters the clerical state and is incardinated into a diocese. An ordained woman member of a religious order or institute would irrevocably change the nature of that order or institute to mixed clerical and lay, a potentiality addressed in detail later.

In view of the above, the question might not be whether ordained women deacons predict women priests. If the Church believes its own teachings, that is not possible. Rather, the question appears to be whether to admit women to the clerical state.

## WHAT DOES ORDINATION MEAN?

So the questions arise: What does ordination mean? What difference does it make whether a woman is or is not ordained? The initial answer is perhaps obvious: through holy orders, the newly ordained receives the grace and charism of the sacrament.

The distinction between the ordained and the unordained is one on which the Church has based an entire theology of orders. Catholic teaching is that there is an ontological distinction between the ordained and unordained. Do opponents to the prospect of ordained women deacons suggest that the ontological distinctions of ordained and unordained do not exist? Catholic teaching is that the ordained have different roles from the unordained. Do opponents to the prospect of ordained women deacons suggest that the roles of the ordained and unordained are interchangeable? Catholic teaching has restated the fact and place of the diaconate within the hierarchy. Do opponents to the prospect of ordained women deacons suggest that the diaconate as an ordained rank in the hierarchy is unnecessary? Clearly, the answer to these and to any questions relative to Catholic understanding of the sacrament of orders and the ministry of the diaconate is no; but equally clearly do opponents mince words when the possibility of ordained women arises as the natural and logical conclusion of the trajectory of history and of ministry by women.

Again: What difference does it make whether a woman is ordained or not? One answer—the theological answer—is clear. The sacrament of orders imparts an indelible ontological distinction upon the person ordained. The question of an ordained woman is not about what she can do, but, rather, about who she is. This point will be examined further after considering the practical implications of ordained women deacons because, as we must recall, an ordained woman deacon is a cleric.

Practical considerations present a response to Cardinal Kasper's dismissal of the need for ordained women deacons because women already fulfill many diaconal roles. What can an ordained woman do that an unordained woman cannot? The question is perhaps better posited: What can a cleric do that a non-cleric cannot? The Church has determined that diaconal ordination is the ordinary means of entering the clerical state, and the clerical state is typically the necessary state for obtaining (being appointed to) office in the Church. That is, there are certain things women can do that appear diaconal by their very nature. But, in no case can an unordained woman—or man—formally obtain offices for which the clerical state is required, nor can she perform certain functions of other offices to which she might be appointed that require clerical status.

## DIACONAL MINISTRY

The functions of offices that require the clerical state often come to the heart of the ministry of the deacon who— ordained to the Word, the liturgy, and charity—is most clearly understood in a parish setting. The parish deacon might well manage the charitable and/or financial affairs of the parish. The parish deacon also might manage classes for catechumens and marriage preparation. But sacramental ministry is also part of the charge of the parish deacon. For example, the ordinary minister of baptism and marriage is the pastor of the parish in which the event takes place. The pastor may delegate another cleric—either someone on his staff or an accredited visitor—to perform the ceremony in his name, and that cleric's name is registered in the parish register as officially acting on behalf of the pastor. The process is simpler if the cleric who is not the pastor is assigned to the parish. Specific note is made if the cleric is a visitor from outside the parish staff. Clearly, deacons can be assigned to parishes, and they ordinarily and often baptize and witness marriages. And deacons can, as visiting clerics, baptize and witness marriages with the pastor's permission.

So, in these cases, can an unordained woman (or man) do everything a deacon can?

Technically, the answer is yes—almost. Anyone can baptize in emergencies—the typical example is the delivery-room nurse or doctor. Further, a layperson can baptize if authorized by the bishop, and can witness marriage in cases of necessity where the proper permission or rescript has been obtained. That is, the bishop can grant special permission to a layperson to baptize within the parish setting, and Rome can grant a rescript for a bishop to allow laypersons to witness marriages within the parish.

In the case of baptism, the diocesan bishop has it within his powers to allow laypersons to baptize.[19] In the case of the need for laypersons to witness marriages, the request must go to Rome. Typically, an individual bishop will state his case to his territorial conference of bishops, which will collectively determine whether their province needs such rescripts. Once this hurdle is cleared, the diocesan bishop will request a rescript to allow for one of two possibilities: ability to nominate laypersons to witness marriages on either ordinary (ongoing) or extraordinary (case-by-case) bases. The rescripts allowing the diocesan bishop to name laypersons to witness marriage are not permanent, but are issued on a five-year renewable basis. In some far-flung and inaccessible territories—for example, in Alaska—the diocesan bishop has been able to name a handful of laypersons as ordinary ministers of baptism and marriage.

The simple example of ministers of baptism and of marriage above is just one of other, similar situations, where the ordinary ministry of the woman deacon could supply for the needs of the people, and the diocesan bishop would not have to have recourse to someone not within his "household"— that is, a non-cleric—to perform ministry.

While a layperson representing the pastor and officiating at the sacraments of baptism and marriage is possible—although improbable in the current context, except in missionary or similarly underserved territories—certain functions are definitively restricted to clerics, be they deacons, priests, or bishops. Two that speak to the heart of the matter are preaching and judging. No layperson may preach at a public Sunday Eucharist,[20] or serve as a single judge, or sign a judgment in, or a dispensation resulting from, a Church legal proceeding. In none of these situations can a diocesan bishop delegate a non-cleric; such delegation is simply refused by canon law.[21]

So it is clear that Cardinal Kasper's offhand dismissal of ordained women deacons—that they already do everything they might do if ordained—is not only incorrect, but also calls into question the revival of the diaconate as a permanent order. The examples above serve as proof text that there is much deacons may do ordinarily that a layperson can do only in the most extraordinary and limited circumstances, or not do at all.

## DIACONAL IDENTITY

Examples of what a deacon may do that a layperson cannot speak only to the functionality of the ordained, not to the public and permanent dedication of their lives to sacred ministry, and the acceptance and ratification of that sacred ministry at the hands of the diocesan bishop. As stated above, the theology of orders, and not functionality, should drive the notion of the diaconate. Realistically, the good works and a majority of the liturgical and sacramental duties of the deacon can, in fact, be undertaken by unordained persons. But Catholic theology argues that the sacrament imparts an indelible ontological distinction upon the person ordained to the diaconate, marking that individual as the person serving *in persona Christi servi*—in the person of Christ, servant. The question of ordained women is not about function, but, rather, about identity. Can a woman take on the diaconal identity, now clearly defined (and codified) as *in persona Christi servi*?

The distinctions between priesthood and diaconate are important here. The deacon serves *in persona Christi servi*. The priest serves *in persona Christi Capitis Ecclesiae*, in the person of Christ, head of the Church. There are no persuasive arguments against a woman serving *in persona Christi servi*—to do so is to reduce sacramental theology to a naive physicalism that denies the mystery of the incarnation. God became human as a male, yes, but the extraordinary point of the incarnation is that God entered history as a *human*. Hence, the *in persona Christi* argument has not withstood the scrutiny of many serious theologians, even as it is clung to by some others.[22]

I posit that this argument or objection to the ordination of women as priests stems not from an understanding of sacramental theology but, rather, from a false notion of the priest, combined with historical superstitions regarding menstruation—superstitions that historically affected the continuance of women in the diaconate. That is, while the so-called iconic argument states that only a male can represent Christ, in fact, it states that only a male can be the icon of priest as currently understood and accepted by the society of the Church. As such, the priesthood is closed to women, not because they cannot represent Christ, but because they cannot represent the Church's understanding of priest. Further, women cannot represent the Church's understanding of priest because the priest and the priest alone (in this schema) touches the sacred, which women—particularly menstruating women—would defile.[23]

However, the magisterial teaching that the Church does not have the authority from Christ to ordain women to the priesthood forms an irreducible argument against the ordination of women as priests. The ordaining prelate must "intend to do as the Church does" in administering the sacrament, and he cannot simultaneously intend to ordain a woman and also intend to do as the Church does.

But there are no such barriers to the ordination of women as deacons, beyond the superstitions surrounding menstruation. The argument from authority does not apply, because the Church itself put forth those understood as the first deacons, who were ordained to service by the apostles. Neither, as delimited above, does the iconic argument apply.

What is at serious risk in the contemporary Church, however, is the development of a male icon of deacon. That is, while canon law now clearly states (following the earlier distinction of the *Catechism*) that the priest and the bishop act in a manner distinct from the deacon, the entire cadre of deacons in the world is male. So, as the Church recovers the diaconate, it reexperiences only the male portion of the diaconate and in so doing may be becoming culturally conditioned to a male-only diaconate.

That is, whether the Church has the authority to restore women to the diaconate is not really in question, but the accretion of experiences and the passing of time could solidify the diaconate as a male-only order. Hence, the question risks becoming "Can a woman take on the identity of the culturally understood male diaconate?" Rather, the question should be "Can a woman take on the core diaconal identity?"

To put it another way, diaconal *service* (functionality) is equally available to men and to women, with limitations, with or without ordination. But diaconal *identity* is rooted in the ontology of orders and lived through a life rooted in prayer. Diaconal service, ordained or not, is *merely* functional when detached from a life lived in God, understood as a regular and ordered life of prayer. That life of prayer creates the identity of the minister (again, ordained or not), and drives the life of service. When the function of the individual, even the function of the ordained individual, is disconnected from a life of prayer, that function (no matter how worthy) is ultimately sterile in that it is disconnected from the life of God in the Church. So the essential point in the identity of the deacon is not his—or her—functionality, but, rather a diaconal identity rooted in a life of prayer. Of course, valid sacramental ordination, not the relative condition of the celebrant's prayer life, makes for valid sacraments, but it is the life rooted in prayer and strengthened by the grace of the sacrament that first identifies the deacon as a minister.

Without question women can live and have lived deeply prayerful lives of diaconal service in the Church as lay ministers. Most of the lay ministers known in the Church in the United States up to the twentieth century were members of apostolic or monastic religious communities of women, whose lives of prayer drove their lives of service. Their public identity as women religious, particularly prior to the reintroduction of the permanent diaconate in the years following the Second Vatican Council, lent some confusion to their connection with the hierarchy. While religious life is a public state within the Church, it is simply a specific way of living Christian life and is by definition not clerical. While some men's religious institutes and orders are mixed clerical and lay (priests, deacons, and brothers), and some men's institutes and orders are wholly clerical or wholly lay, women's institutes and orders are wholly lay (sisters and nuns).

Most apostolic institutes and noncontemplative monastic orders of women in the United States perform what in other terms is diaconal ministry. It is by their diminution and diminishment that women religious are now recognized as having borne the majority of diaconal service in the United States; the ministries once carried out by women religious are dying out. The concurrent expansion of (predominantly female) lay ecclesial ministry supports the view that women are perhaps more identified with the ministry of service than men. In fact, one can argue that women (especially apostolic women religious) are more representative of the diaconal identity as one of prayer and service, whereas men (specifically ordained male deacons) are more identified with diaconal functionality where it is understood as the ministry of the liturgy.

For men or for women, the tripartite diaconal call to service—to the Word, to the liturgy, and to charity—must be carefully balanced to achieve a clear diaconal identity. That careful balance, and that diaconal identity, ought to be available to both.

## WHY IS THE ORDINATION OF WOMEN GOOD AND NECESSARY?

The ordination of women to the diaconate cannot and will not replace monastic or apostolic religious life for women. But the ordained diaconate of women can coexist with women's religious life, inside or outside institutes and orders. The complex history of women's religious life demonstrates at least two ritually acknowledged events: permanent membership and personal consecration, which are sometimes combined in a single ceremony whereby vows of poverty, chastity, and obedience are professed. Separately, the personal consecration of the individual sister to God is sometimes ceremonially recognized by "veiling" or, rarely, consecration to a life of virginity. Apostolic women religious typically profess vows of poverty, chastity, and obedience, according to the constitutions of their institutes. The constitutions delimit the way religious life will be led, but are sufficient indication that ministerial work will be what otherwise would be recognized as diaconal service. That is, vows are typically pronounced to be lived according to the constitutions of a given institute, which equally typically point to a particular work or works.

Only slight remnants of diaconal ordination ceremonies remain in the profession ceremonies of apostolic women religious, although the ceremonies for contemplative nuns seem to echo more of that tradition. Approximately four years after monastic profession, Carthusian nuns may receive the consecration of a virgin in a ceremony specific to their order that appears to include remnants of a diaconal ordination ceremony. In that ceremony the Carthusian nun receives a stole, a maniple, and a small cross on her shoulder.[24] The Carthusian ceremonial is hundreds of years old, but, contemporaneously, the early habit of the Religious of the Assumption—founded at Paris in 1839 by Saint Marie Eugénie Milleret (1817–98) and originally dedicated to education—includes a white chapel mantle with a violet cross on the shoulder, perhaps an intuitive remnant of the earlier ceremonies and indicative of dedication to a service now recognized as diaconal.

Ceremonials aside, many contemporary women clearly serve the Church in diaconal roles. Significant numbers of women still seek lives of prayer and service in apostolic, monastic, and contemplative communities. Others, however, choose to live as seculars (married or single) dedicated to lay ecclesial ministry. Within this huge cadre of women ministers—religious and secular—there are individual women well suited and, arguably, called to the ordained diaconate. Equally, it must be noted, there are women who do not wish to become involved in the clerical system and prefer to retain their lay ministerial status, either as religious or secular lay ecclesial ministers. Others prefer lay status while working within various not-for-profit organizations, including various ministries controlled by religious institutes.

But there are significant numbers of women who would prefer to have the specific relationship to the bishop that clerical status commands, as well as the public identity of deacon. There are also significant numbers of people who would welcome the diaconal ministry of women—in chaplaincies, social services, and ecclesiastical offices. The fact of the matter is, it is a new world. In developed countries at least, women are respected as intellectual and spiritual equals to men. Women are valued professionals as well as wives and mothers. Women are role models for the girls who come behind them. And women make up more than half of the billion or so Catholics in the world.

The question of why the ordination of women is good and necessary becomes "What will ordination of women say about the nature of the Church and the exercise of ministry?" In too many quarters, the Catholic Church is derided and despised for its perceived views of women. The entire laundry list of so-called women's issues clouds the crying need of the people of God for ministry by women. Unfortunately, some of the very women who might provide for such ministry are caught up in these other issues—abortion, birth control, and so forth—even as they rail against the horrors of priestly pederasty and concomitant episcopal cover-ups, the scandal of human trafficking, and the world's willful ignorance of the genuine needs for women's and children's nutrition and health care.

The conflation of issues—those the Church considers legitimate and those the Church opposes—may in fact be a side of the multifaceted problem that too many in the hierarchy have with women. A thin wedge of antifeminism began to split the Church male and female as early as the fourth century, some say earlier. That split continued to the first millennium. The eleventh and twelfth centuries demonstrated a greater widening of the gap, so that in terms of ministry there began and now remains a defined split between the men and women of the Church. The disparate professional training for many men and for women entering ministry today only encourages and solidifies that split. Specifically, men on a path to ordination, including the diaconate, are educated and trained in a manner distinct from (and predominantly apart from) women preparing for lay ministry.

Many generous individuals—male and female—want to devote their lives to Church service, but only the few celibate males in priestly formation are provided with years of leisure to study the philosophy and theology necessary for priesthood. While many other men and women study and train for ministry, often they study theology without an underpinning of philosophy. As a result, some men and more women enter lay ministry with deficient (or at least unequal) education and training. The problem becomes a self-feeding and unending syllogism that proves the intent of the argument against ordained women deacons: Because laywomen are often improperly educated, they therefore incorrectly understand Catholic doctrine; such women cannot be trusted in Church assignments. Because women cannot be trusted in Church assignments, women should not be ordained.

Of course, there is plenty wrong with that syllogism, but

the theme is clear: Women cannot be educated sufficiently for ordination, and so they should not be educated for ordination because "we" (the hierarchy) do not want to ordain them. Such is nearly the logic of the 2001 notification mentioned earlier, which essentially directs bishops not to train women for diaconal ordination because "we" do not see that "we" will be ordaining them.

But the ordination of women is both good and necessary, because the Church, to borrow John Paul II's image, must breathe "with two lungs"—the male and the female—in the diaconate. The ministry of service that comprises the diaconate is not specifically male—or female—but it is, specifically, a ministry of service. If we take the analogy of apostolic women religious in the United States—of whom fewer than 60,000 remain—we can see that the traditional diaconal works they undertook are fading, dying, and being absorbed into other entities. Institutionally, these include hospitals, orphanages, educational institutions, even retreat houses and day-care centers. On the diocesan and parish level, these include religious education and sacramental preparation, as well as visiting the sick, consoling the bereaved, and facilitating a sense of community. Many of these diaconal functions, undertaken throughout the modern era by apostolic women religious, are now entered into by a cadre of men ordained to the order of deacon. They are also entered into by male and female lay ecclesial ministers. But the Church needs more ordained ministers. Is it possible to reconsider the historicity of the female diaconate?

## A NOTE ABOUT HISTORY

The historical debate about women deacons weaves together arguments about the facts surrounding their appointment (whether by ordination or by some other means), their functions, and their very existence. Most modern historical debates begin with one of two premises: women were ordained, or women were not ordained.[25] But, what is ordination? The simple understanding is that ordination comes after the determination by the diocesan bishop that an individual is qualified for service: for our purposes here, qualified for diaconal service *in persona Christi.*

The historical evidence ably presented by Gary Macy in this volume, and by others elsewhere, clearly demonstrates that women were deacons. They were called deacons, they were named such by bishops, and they served diaconal functions. Yet, despite the existence of ancient conciliar canons, medieval papal letters, and a substantial number of ordination ceremonies (East and West), some argued centuries after the fact that those women ordained as deacons did not receive sacramental ordination. What is not often recalled is that the preponderance of women ordained as deacons were so ordained before the solidification of sacramental theology, which took place concurrent with the fading of the diaconate.

It appears that the trajectory of thought aimed at disregarding the historical evidence of the ordination of women as deacons is twofold: first, early ordinations of women were not sacramental ordinations (independent of the intent of the ordaining bishop) because women cannot receive the sacrament of orders, as in the objections of Gratian mentioned earlier; or, second, no diaconal ordination (of a man or a woman) is or ever was a sacramental ordination. As has been presented earlier in this volume, however, more recent scholarship and Church teaching defines ordination to the diaconate as included in the sacrament of orders.

By the time the Church began to define ordination as a sacrament, few persons, other than candidates for priestly ordination, were being ordained in the Western Church. Eastern Churches (Catholic and Orthodox) retained a stronger tradition of the distinct diaconate, and some Orthodox Churches retained the ordination of monastic women deacons, in large part due to the need for a deacon in the liturgy. Yet many Churches, both Eastern and Western not in complete communion with Rome, those whose sacraments and orders the Catholic Church recognizes as valid, have a recent (and in some cases relatively unbroken) tradition of ordaining women to the diaconate.

No definitive statement—positive or negative—has been made by the Holy See regarding the validity of the orders of these women. To affirm the validity of their orders would call into question the Catholic Church's refusal to restore its own female diaconate in both the East and the West. To repudiate the validity of their orders would call into question the Catholic Church's recognition of and agreements with these other Churches. The experiences of these other Churches, however, is illustrative of the female diaconate in the present, and perhaps predictive of how the Catholic Church, particularly the Roman Catholic Church, might incorporate women into its order of deacon.

## WHO WOULD BECOME A DEACON?

What woman would become an ordained Roman Catholic deacon? For some women the very idea of ordination, of becoming directly and irrevocably involved in the clerical caste, is unthinkable. These very women remain dedicated to service of the people of God through the ministries of the Catholic Church, and their service can echo that of the permanent deacon. The majority of these women are apostolic religious who see their consecrated life as a means of prophetic witness outside "the system." That is, while they are publicly identified as vowed religious, they are not clerics; technically, they are laypersons. Although they have special identities delineated by canon law, their consecrations are extensions of their baptismal promises. They are not, nor do they wish to become, ordained.

Many of the ministries of these women religious are self-funded, either through their institutes or institute-owned organizations. Many of them work for non-Church-related entities in a variety of positions, often as social workers, attorneys, or teachers. Some devote their lives to public advocacy, for example, through nongovernmental organizations (NGOs) accredited to the United Nations. Many of these might find clerical status in conflict with the freedom to speak and write as they wish, even though they are still bound in obedience to their religious superiors and, by extension, to the law of the Church. Further, the corporate ministries of their institutes (and their very presence in a diocese) depend upon the implicit or explicit permission of the diocesan bishop.

Other apostolic women religious, who work and minister directly for diocesan entities, including parishes, might find diaconal ordination beneficial to their work. While their dedication to ministry is lived through the constitutions or rule of their institutes or orders, their choosing ordination would not be redundant but enhancing. Such ordination would enable them to receive faculties from their bishop, most notably for preaching, but also for baptizing and witnessing marriages. They would also be eligible to be single judges in canonical trials, to sign ecclesial legal proceedings, and to obtain office.

A cadre of women who might choose to remain in unordained ministry is comprised of the thousands of lay ecclesial ministers who believe themselves not called to the diaconate, and who prefer to remain lay ecclesial ministers. This group is of deep interest here because it includes primarily women not called to consecrated life (as religious, consecrated virgins, hermits, or members of secular institutes), yet who minister professionally in some Church entity, be it at the parish, diocesan, or national level. Those who are formally named, and in some cases certified, by their bishops as lay ecclesial ministers may have completed professional training much like that of the contemporary deacon. They have undergone formation and training in the spiritual, human, intellectual, and professional areas of development delineated by the United States Conference of Catholic Bishops as necessary to lay ecclesial ministry. Some may have been formally appointed by their bishops as lay ecclesial ministers in a public ceremony.

While many lay ecclesial ministers—married or celibate, and neither publicly vowed nor consecrated—would choose to remain as unordained ministers within whatever setting or structure they find themselves, others might seek ordination to the diaconate. Of course, no one self-elects to become a deacon. The vocation to the diaconate—as with any other vocation—is one that must be examined and tested.

## WHAT WOULD THE CHURCH LOOK LIKE WITH WOMEN DEACONS?

A major barrier to the reintroduction of women to the permanent diaconate is that no one really knows how it would work. What would a woman ordained as deacon do? Would she be married or celibate? Might she be a professed religious? How would she be supported? Where would she live?

The permanent diaconate including women would look much like the permanent diaconate of today in terms of functionality, with certain distinctions—most important, that women deacon would be particularly able to bring the Word, the liturgy, and charity directly to other women. As with the women who were deacons in the ancient church, they would minister to sick and dying women and be available to all manner of vulnerable women. They would make the ministry of the Church—the ministry of Jesus—available to women (and men) in a new-old way.

In the ancient world, intimate ministry by men to women was unseemly; in the contemporary world such is often equally unseemly, and uncomfortable. Epiphanius, a church father known for his orthodoxy, wrote in the fourth century that women deacons ministered to sick and dying women precisely because such ministry would be unseemly if carried out by a man. Recognizing that one of the reasons given for restoring monastic women deacons in the Orthodox Church of Greece followed Epiphanius' reasoning, it is obvious that there are restrictions and reticences between unmarried, unrelated, women and men.[26]

Ministry to the sick and dying is a primary case in point. All persons are particularly vulnerable when injured or ill. Whether they are hospitalized or not, their dignity is endangered by their lack of privacy and inability to care for themselves. Conscious, semiconscious, or unconscious, these persons are often unable to control access to their presence or to their very bodies. Propriety calls for the availability of ministry by women, ministry that involves far more than brief sacramental encounters, no matter how beneficial or necessary, performed by priests.

Phyllis Zagano

There are significant numbers of women lay ecclesial ministers (religious and secular) who offer chaplaincy services through hospitals, hospices, and home-care agencies. Many have completed a rigorous course of certification as health-care chaplains. Would it make any difference if any of these women—religious or secular—were to be ordained as deacons? Perhaps the first place to look for an answer is the experience of ordained deacons who are certified Catholic health-care chaplains. Does the grace and charism of order distinguish *their* ministries? In direct chaplaincy to the ill, there is little a deacon can do that an unordained person cannot do. It is important to recognize, however, that modern sacramental practice does not often distinguish between the sacrament of the sick and the sacrament of reconciliation, despite their being distinct sacraments. Current theory holds to the remission of sin being possible through anointing alone, and perhaps because of this, the Congregation for the Doctrine of the Faith (following determinations of the Council of Trent) issued a "Note on the Minister of the Anointing of the Sick," stating that only a priest may anoint sacramentally and that such is to be held definitively. The Note specifically excludes both deacons and laypersons, stating they cannot be delegated to administer the sacrament.[27]

Not all women ordained to the diaconate would become full-time health-care chaplains. In fact, not all women ordained to the diaconate would become full-time deacons. Like their male counterparts, they would at ordination become incardinated to the diocese of their ordaining diocesan bishop. While patterns vary around the world, all women ordained to the diaconate would become incardinated to a diocese, excepting those who belong to religious institutes or orders.[28] During the ordination ceremony, the candidate for the permanent diaconate promises obedience and respect to the diocesan bishop and his successors (secular deacons are ordained by their diocesan bishop).

## WOMEN RELIGIOUS ORDAINED TO THE DIACONATE

What about women religious? The line of authority is clear for secular deacon candidates: they become clerics incardinated in a geographical diocese. Women religious, already promised in obedience to their religious superiors, present a difficult situation. When men religious are ordained to the diaconate or the priesthood, they already have a clerical general superior who acts as the equivalent of a bishop as regards their clerical status. In the case of mixed clerical and lay institutes and orders, only a priest may hold the office of general superior, as no layperson may have jurisdiction over a cleric.

However, if a woman religious were ordained to the diaconate, she would present a canonical conundrum for her superiors. First, of course, she would need the permission of her general superior to be ordained. Further, her institute or order would have to have made a prior determination to become a mixed clerical and lay group. Having made that determination, and recalling that no layperson may have jurisdiction over a cleric, the institute or order might thereby restrict itself in its choice of general superiors. It is unknown whether mixed clerical and lay institutes and orders could have nonclerical general superiors where the only clerical members are deacons. If that restriction cannot be effectively dealt with, or if the given group chooses not to become mixed clerical and lay, or if the general superior refuses permission for ordination, then the woman religious deacon candidate would have to choose between her religious community and ordination.

The constraints levied by the requirement for an ordained superior are in theory lessened in territorial abbeys of women, where territorial abbesses historically held absolute authority, even over clerics.[29] While their authority does not extend to ordination, it does extend to the effective granting of faculties: no cleric celebrates sacraments or preaches within an abbey's territory without the permission of the abbess (or abbot). Hence, there is historical precedent and current practice that might encourage the understanding that the quasi-episcopal authority of an abbess, combined with her receipt of perpetual profession, would suffice for the "incardination" of a member of her abbey who would be ordained a deacon.[30] Or, alternatively, any member of the abbey or monastery elected as abbess (or prioress) would also be ordained to the diaconate.[31] (Again, recall the findings of the Holy Synod of the Orthodox Church of Greece regarding monastic women deacons.)

The canonical conundrum regarding the ordaining of women religious as deacons is real and recalls other distinctions in religious life for women. For the purposes of this discussion, distinct categories of women religious must be understood. For the most part, women religious are considered either "nuns" or "sisters."

While the 1983 Code of Canon Law no longer stipulates solemn vows, women who live cloistered lives in monasteries and abbeys are called nuns. (The new Code says only that vows are considered solemn where the Church recognizes them as such.)[32] The chief distinction is that those who profess solemn vows renounce all ownership of property.

Other women religious are called sisters. Some belong to institutes living one or another major charism—Franciscan, Dominican, Benedictine—or they belong to any of the many institutes founded in modern times. Of these, some are "diocesan right" and some are "pontifical right." That is, some have been founded within the territory of and by leave of (or even at the request of) the diocesan bishop. These are known as diocesan institutes. Pontifical institutes may have been founded in a similar fashion, but they are not in the charge of the diocesan bishop, except as regards the fact of their ministry within his diocese.

So, for women religious, there are three modes: territorial abbeys and monasteries (including cloistered monasteries), diocesan institutes, and pontifical institutes. Among these, an argument can be made for the quasi-episcopal status of the territorial abbess. Both diocesan and pontifical institutes, however, are headed by laywomen.

Diocesan institutes present an interesting case. Until the promulgation of the 1917 Code of Canon Law, diocesan bishops had the right to admit women to diocesan institutes. Was this practice a vestige of a bishop in the early Church calling forth women to serve as deacons within his diocese? For over three hundred years, women religious have responded to invitations of diocesan bishops to found religious houses in the United States. As the diocesan system strengthened in the United States (until 1908, the United States was considered a mission territory), the preponderance of newly founded institutes served specifically diocesan ministries: parochial schools, parish catechesis, other parish-based ministries, and diocesan-wide endeavors such as Catholic charities, hospitals, nursing homes, and work within diocesan headquarters. Were these women religious the deacons American bishops intuitively needed?

Pontifical institutes are similarly interesting. They are not in the charge of the diocesan bishop but, rather, respond to the authority of the pope via the Congregation for Institutes of Consecrated Life and Societies of Apostolic Life

(CICLSAL).[33] Even so, as with men's religious institutes and orders, pontifical institutes operate within a diocese only by permission of its local ordinary. Their charisms equally display a diaconal character: they own and operate all levels of educational institutions, hospitals, and social service agencies, and their members are individually employed in parish and diocesan ministries.

The complex history of women religious in the United States cannot be told here, but in general it serves as example of the concept that bishops needed diaconal service and that they called on women religious to provide that service. In any event, a woman member of a religious order or institute that determined that it would be mixed clerical and lay would need the permission of her provincial or general superior to accept ordination to the diaconate, which permission would only be given by advice, or possibly consent, of her unit's council.[34]

Should a women's religious institute choose not to become mixed clerical and lay, or should an individual religious be refused permission to be ordained within her institute, there is always the possibility that a new religious institute of women could be founded: either mixed clerical and lay or wholly clerical. A wholly clerical institute of women religious would obviate the question of who might be eligible to be elected as general superior, whereas a new mixed clerical and lay institute would ostensibly have to determine at its founding that its superiors would be chosen from among the ordained, or be willing to be ordained if chosen.[35]

## SECULAR WOMEN ORDAINED TO THE DIACONATE

As noted above, a secular woman ordained to the diaconate becomes incardinated into the diocese of her ordaining bishop, just as a secular male deacon does. And just as he does, she promises obedience and respect to her diocesan bishop and his successors. Included is her promise to be obedient to the law of the Church, which allows married men to be ordained deacons, but does not allow ordained men to contract a marriage. The stipulation would carry over to women: married women could be ordained deacons, but ordained women could not contract a marriage.

A married man who is a candidate for ordination must present a petition from his wife in support of his own petition for ordination. In most dioceses of the United States, wives attend pre-ordination classes with their husbands (although in some dioceses they are refused permission to speak in class). Wives also attend pre-ordination retreats and gatherings. The first guidelines for diaconal formation and ministry issued by the United States Conference of Catholic Bishops required (1) that wives formally consent to their husbands' ordination; (2) that wives may freely determine the extent to which they participate in the ministry; (3) that wives have developmental programs; (4) that bishops consider familial economic situations; (5) that all understand that familial commitments take priority over ministry; and (6) that wives have open communications with the diocesan diaconate office. These requirements remain in practice, with perhaps more emphasis on the involvement of older children of deacon families in formation and other programs, where appropriate.[36]

The role of the deacon's wife is variously understood from diocese to diocese and from diaconal family to diaconal family, and her role is continually emerging. Significant research has been undertaken, and continues, but one constant (anecdotally, at least) is this question: If the two are one flesh in marriage, how is it that only one may be ordained to ministry, especially since each has undergone the same training program?[37]

Confusing, even difficult, as the role of the deacon's wife may be, the role of the deacon's husband would be analogous to it only to a certain extent. That is, magisterial documents still speak of the husband as "head" of the household. Despite the spousal permission needed for a man to be accepted as a candidate for diaconal orders, there remains a cultural understanding within the Church that wives accede to their husband's career choices and all they may entail.

I recognize that the vocation to the diaconate is not a "career," but I believe the principle holds. What happens, then, when things are reversed? What happens when a wife wants to become a deacon? She would need the permissive agreement of her husband to enter into formation and training, and to accept eventual ordination. But how might the Church think about a married woman promised in obedience to her bishop? The culture is not accustomed to such dual relationships, even as it does not consider the necessary obedience to the bishop as interfering with the marriage of a male deacon.

It is perhaps for this reason that, when he recommended the restoration of women to the diaconate during the Second Vatican Council, Italian Bishop Giuseppe Ruotolo recommended that such ordination be limited to celibate women. His concept brings us in two directions: unmarried women, religious and secular. The complications of ordination for women religious are as outlined above. What are the complications for secular unmarried women?

To begin with, while the deacon at ordination promises obedience to the bishop, and is permanently bound through incardination to that bishop's diocese, there is no promise of subsidy from the bishop to the deacon. That is, while the deacon is permanently bound—in theory, at least—to the "bishop's household," the bishop is not required to provide any form of support to the deacon. In fact, the diaconate (at least in the contemporary West) is in large part a volunteer ministry. So the deacon candidate must effectively provide for his—or her—own support in whatever way possible. The bishop is not bound to provide employment or housing. Further, deacons are not eligible for Mass stipends (as they do not celebrate the Eucharist), nor are they typically the recipients of "stole fees" for performing marriages or baptisms. So their ministry is either self-supporting or supported by an employment contract with a parish or diocese or with another nonecclesial entity.

A candidate for the permanent diaconate in the United States must be at least thirty-five years of age, but if we consider the falling numbers of vocations to feminine religious life and the concurrent meteoric rise in vocations to lay ecclesial ministry (of which approximately 85 percent are women), it is entirely possible that young—or at least younger—unmarried women might choose the permanent diaconate as a vocation early in life.[38] What implications does this have for the bishop? The few male secular celibate deacons in developed nations can, if necessary, find housing in parish rectories, often the parishes where they are employed either generally as deacons or specifically as catechists. The fact of rectory room and board can support their full-time, if low-paid, ministry.

But what about the women? A young woman choosing lay ecclesial ministry is free to marry; a young woman ordained to the diaconate would not be.[39] But a young woman who chooses celibacy would be well advised to find a permanent relationship in life to support her ministry. At present the only available avenue is religious life. But religious life for women might not admit to clerical members. Further, the starting point in vocational discernment to religious life is personal consecration to God, not ministry or community life for the purpose of supporting ministry.

As noted above, one possibility would be a new form of religious institute, founded specifically to allow for women deacons. Realistically, such a group might be the only way to guarantee the future of the celibate young woman who wishes to be ordained a deacon, although it does not completely answer the very practical questions as to how secular community life and disparate diaconal ministries could be combined. The diaconate is not, after all, apostolic religious life.

To be sure, older widowed or never-married women might also find themselves called to the diaconate, and their age ranges would be more in keeping with the current cadre of men deacon candidates, at least in the United States. These women may already have careers or inheritances to support the essentially volunteer ministry of the diaconate. History points out that the minimum age for a woman deacon dropped from sixty to forty,[40] the present general age range of a number of second-career or adjunct-career lay ministers of both genders.

The practicalities of returning women to the diaconate are complex, but the underlying support—the only genuine reason for the Church to restore women to ordained diaconal service—is the needs of the Church.

## DOES THE CHURCH NEED WOMEN DEACONS?

To answer this question, particularly in light of the practical obstacles outlined above, the discussion must return to Cardinal Kasper's initial response: Women can already do everything a deacon can do. Well, they can't. An unordained woman cannot preach at a public liturgy—and even a bishop cannot give her (or any unordained person) permission to do so. An unordained woman cannot be a single judge on a tribunal. Nor can she easily be an ordinary minister of baptism, or an ordinary witness to marriage. An unordained woman cannot obtain certain offices in the Church—or at least she cannot fully function in them if she happens to hold the position. The work of many women who hold Church offices would be strengthened by their entering the clerical state as deacons—women are chancellors, tribunal judges, and parish administrators. Further, women deacons would be able to preach at Eucharistic liturgies, baptize, and witness marriages—and they would be trained and educated to do so by their bishops.

Most important, the Church is desperately in need of the ministry of service the diaconate provides, and women deacons could reasonably be expected to take up the traditional diaconal works now defining the permanent diaconate: catechesis, chaplaincy, social services. That women have continually performed these works over the centuries provides heft to the trajectory of history that now brings women back to the earliest call to service. Women have provided these and similar ministries throughout history, especially for other women. There seems no reason not to circle back to this natural historical development.

The simple question is: Would the Church benefit from the restoration of women to the diaconate? There are no guarantees, but if the ministry of discernment is to be taken to heart, one must answer in the affirmative.

# NOTES

## INTRODUCTION

1. Cardinal Giacomo Antonelli (1806–76) entered the diplomatic service of Pope Gregory XVI as a layman in 1836, was ordained deacon in 1840, and was created a cardinal in 1847. He oversaw temporal affairs for Pius IX and was made Vatican secretary of state in 1848. Cardinal Teodolfo Mertel (1806–99) entered papal service as a layman and was subsequently ordained deacon by Pius IX in 1858. Frank J. Coppa, *Cardinal Giacomo Antonelli and Papal Politics in European Affairs* (Albany: State University of New York Press, 1990); "Cardinaux créés par Pie IX," *Annuaire Pontifical Catholique de 1904* (Paris: Maison de la Bonne Presse, 1905), 209.

2. Cipriano Vagaggini, "L'ordinazione delle diaconesse nella tradizione greca e bizantina," *Orientalia christiana periodica* 40 (1974): 149–89. The suppression of Vagaggini's study as a Vatican document is noted in Peter Hebblethwaite, *Paul VI: The First Modern Pope* (New York and Mahwah, NJ: Paulist Press, 1993), 640.

3. Roger Gryson, *The Ministry of Women in the Early Church* (Collegeville, MN: Liturgical Press, 1976); Aimé Georges Martimort, *Deaconesses: An Historical Study* (San Francisco: Ignatius Press, 1986). Each appeared earlier in French.

4. Evangelos Theodorou, *Heroines of Love: Deaconesses through the Ages* (Athens: Apostlika Diakonia of the Church of Greece, 1949), and *The "Ordination" or "Appointment" of Deaconesses* (Athens, 1954); Kyriaki Karidoyanes FitzGerald,

*Women Deacons in the Orthodox Church: Called to Holiness and Ministry* (Brookline, MA: Holy Cross Orthodox Press, 1998); Phyllis Zagano, *Holy Saturday: An Argument for the Restoration of the Female Diaconate in the Catholic Church* (New York: Crossroad/Herder, 2000).

5. Ute Eisen, *Women Officeholders in Early Christianity: Epigraphical and Literary Studies* (Collegeville, MN: Liturgical Press, 2000).

6. J. N. M. Wijngaards, *No Women in Holy Orders? The Women Deacons of the Early Church* (Norwich, UK: Canterbury Press, 2002), and *Women Deacons in the Early Church: Historical Texts and Contemporary Debates* (New York: Crossroad, 2006).

7. Kevin Madigan and Carolyn Osiek, *Ordained Women in the Early Church: A Documentary History* (Baltimore: Johns Hopkins Press, 2005); *Gary Macy, The Hidden History of Women's Ordination: Female Clergy in the Medieval West* (New York: Oxford University Press, 2008).

## WOMEN DEACONS: HISTORY

1. For the most part, references are to easily available secondary sources that contain the references to the original sources cited in the text.

2. Josephine Mayer, *Monumenta de viduis diaconissis virginibusque tractantia, Florilegium patristicum tam veteris quam medii aevi auctores complectens* 42 (Bonn: Peter Hanstein, 1938).

3. Adriana Valerio, *La questione femminile nei secoli X–XII: Una rilettura storica di alcune experienze in Campania* (Naples: D'Auria, 1983).

4. Heike Grierser, Rosemarie Nürnberg, and Gisela Muschiol, "Texte aus der kirchlichen Tradition und lehramtliche

Dokumente," in Peter Hünermann, Albert Biesinger, Marianne Heimbach-Steins, and Anne Jenson, eds., *Diakonat: Ein Amt für Frauen in der Kirche—Ein frauengerechtes Amt?* (Ostfildern: Schwabenverlag, 1997).

5. Ute Eisen, *Women Officeholders in Early Christianity: Epigraphical and Literary Studies* (Collegeville, MN: Liturgical Press, 2000).

6. Kyriaki Karidoyanes FitzGerald, *Women Deacons in the Orthodox Church: Called to Holiness and Ministry*, rev. ed. (Brookline, MA: Holy Cross Orthodox Press, 1999).

7. John Wijngaards, *No Women in Holy Orders? The Women Deacons of the Early Church* (Norwich, UK: Canterbury Press, 2002).

8. Kevin Madigan and Carolyn Osiek, *Ordained Women in the Early Church: A Documentary History* (Baltimore: Johns Hopkins Press, 2005).

9. For a review of the literature on this subject, see Gary Macy, *The Hidden History of Women's Ordination: Female Clergy in the Medieval West* (New York: Oxford University Press, 2008), 1–22. To this list must be added the important study of Cipriano Vagaggini, "L'ordinazione delle diaconesse nella tradizione greca e bizantina," *Orientalia christiana periodica* 40 (1974): 149–89.

10. Madigan and Osiek, *Ordained Women*, 14.

11. Ibid., 14–18.

12. Ibid., 19.

13. Wijngaards, *No Women*, 160.

14. Madigan and Osiek, *Ordained Women*, 19.

15. Ibid., 19–20.

16. Ibid., 20–21.

17. Ibid., 20.

18. On Ambrosiaster's commentary and its influence in Christian theology, see Macy, *Hidden History*, 91–93.

19. On Abelard and his commentary, see Macy, *Hidden History*, 93–96.

20. "Speaking of deacons, [Paul] brings in the women who were called deacons since they minister to priests as [women] were accustomed to do for the apostles and to Jesus himself. [Paul] cautions that they be chosen in the same way as deacons." Macy, *Hidden History*, 96 and 211. Translation is by the author.

21. Madigan and Osiek, *Ordained Women*, 27–28.

22. Ibid., 28–29.

23. Ibid., 32.

24. Ibid., 43–47.

25. Eisen, *Women Officeholders*, 158–98, Madigan and Osiek, *Ordained Women*, 67–96.

26. Madigan and Osiek, *Ordained Women*, 134–35.

27. Ibid., 135.

28. See, e.g., Madigan and Osiek, *Ordained Women*, 184.

29. See Macy, *Hidden History*, 67.

30. Ibid.

31. Ibid., 67–68.

32. Ibid., 68.

33. Ibid., 68–69.

34. Ibid., 69.

35. Ibid.

36. Ibid., 70. The reference to "godmothers" here refers to the medieval practice of considering godparents as close relatives. This statute is forbidding a form of "spiritual incest."

37. Ibid., 69.

38. Ibid.

39. Ibid.

40. Ibid., 70.

41. Ibid., 35. Silva Candida is one of the suburban dioceses of Rome.

42. Ibid. The Leonine City is the part of Rome encompassed by the Leonine Wall, built by Pope Leo IV in the ninth century.

43. Ibid.

44. Ibid.

45. Ibid., 93–96.

46. Madigan and Osiek, *Ordained Women*, 113–14.

47. See Macy, *Hidden History*, 7–8.

48. Ibid., 7. These two terms refer to two different kinds of ritual initiation. χειρτονὶα (*cheirotonia*) refers to ordination in the sense now used for the diaconate and priesthood. χειροφεσὶα (*cheirothesia*) refers to a laying on of hands that accompanies minor orders. Morin's point is that both terms are used for the ordination of both men and women deacons.

49. Wijngaards, *No Women?* 22–44.

50. FitzGerald, *Women Deacons*, 202–4.

51. This section on ordination rites is based on Macy, *Hidden History*, 70–73.

52. Ibid., 70.

53. Ibid., 71.

54. Ibid.

55. Ibid.

56. Before the current revisions to the Roman Pontifical, ordinations usually took place immediately prior to the liturgical function that the newly ordained would perform for the first time. For example, a subdeacon would be ordained just before the Epistle, which he would then read for the first time. A deacon was ordained just before the Gospel, which he would then read for the first time. In this ordination rite, the woman deacon was ordained immediately before the Gospel. This suggests that the woman deacon was expected to do exactly the same as the male deacon: to proclaim the Gospel at Mass. And, in fact, there is good his-

torical evidence to show that women deacons did proclaim the Gospel. See Macy, *Hidden History*, 70–74, 85, 97, 100–103.

57. Cyrille Vogel, *Medieval Liturgy: An Introduction to the Sources*, rev. ed. (Washington, DC: Pastoral Press, 1986), 251.

58. "The practical application of charity was probably the most potent single cause of Christian success." Henry Chadwick, *The Early Church*, rev. ed. (New York: Penguin Books, 1993), 56.

59. The seven men mentioned in Acts are not called deacons and it is only in the second century that they begin to be identified as such. See William Ditewig, *The Emerging Diaconate: Servant Leaders in a Servant Church* (Mahwah, NJ: Paulist Press, 2007), 59.

60. Wijngaards, *No Women*, 173. For a slightly different translation, see Madigan and Osiek, *Ordained Women*, 113.

61. Wijngaards, *No Women*, 162.

62. Ibid., 160.

63. Ibid., 177.

64. Madigan and Osiek, *Ordained Women*, 111.

65. FitzGerald, *Women Deacons*, 204.

66. Macy, *Hidden History*, 97.

67. Ibid., 97–101.

68. This section is taken from Macy, *Hidden History*, 74–80.

69. Jo Ann McNamara, "Chaste Marriage and Clerical Celibacy," in *Sexual Practices and the Medieval Church*, eds. Vern Bullough and Jamyes Brundage (Buffalo, NY: Prometheus Books, 1982), 24.

70. Macy, *Hidden History*, 68–69, 85.

71. Ibid., 64–65.

72. Ibid., 93–96.

73. Mary Martin McLaughlin, "Peter Abelard and the Dignity of Women: Twelfth Century 'Feminism' in Theory and Practice," in *Pierre Abélard Pierre le Vénérable: Les courants philosophiques, littéraires et artistiques en occident au milieu du XIIe siècle* (Paris: Éditions du Centre National de la Recherche Scientifique, 1975), 287–333; and Jean Leclerq, "Ad ipsam sophiam Christum: le témoignage monastique d'Abélard," *Revue d'ascétique et de mystique* xlvi (1970), 161–81.

74. McLaughlin, "Peter Abelard," 294.

75. Madigan and Osiek, *Ordained Women*, 137.

76. Ibid., 136.

77. Ibid., 138. In the funeral oration for his sister Gorgonia, Gregory Nazianzus related how she approached the altar to pray during an illness. See the references and text given by the Medieval Sourcebook, http://www.fordham.edu/halsall/basis/gregnaz-gorgonia.html.

78. For a recent account of this history, see Michel Lauwers, "Les femmes et l'eucharistie dans l'Occident medieval: indertis, transgressions, dévotion eucharistique (XIIe–XVe siècle)," in *Pratiques de l'eucharistie dans les Églises d'Orient et d'Occident Antiquté et Moyen Âge*, 2 vols., eds. Nicole Bériou, Beatrice Caseau, and Dominique Rigaux (Paris: Institute d'Études Augustiniennes, 2009), 1:445–76.

79. For a full discussion of research on the meaning of ordination in the early Church, see Macy, *Hidden History*, 26–35.

80. Yves Congar, "My Path-Findings in the Theology of Laity and Ministries," *The Jurist* 32 (1972): 180.

81. On the change in the definition of ordination in the eleventh through the thirteenth centuries, see Macy, *Hidden History*, 89–110.

82. *Decretum*, C. 15, q. 3, princ., in *Corpus iuris canonici*, 2 vols., ed. Emil Friedberg (Graz: Akademische Druck-und-Verlagsanstalt, 1959), 1:750.

83. Macy, *Hidden History*, 97.

84. Ibid., 97–105.

85. Ibid., 100.

## WOMEN DEACONS: PRESENT POSSIBILITIES

1. It is interesting to remember that at the time of the Second Vatican Council, it would have been a violation of this canon for a bishop knowingly to ordain a "permanent" deacon. That is why Pope Paul VI had to change the law when he implemented the Council's decision with *Sacrum Diaconatus Ordinem* in 1967. Law reflects theology, and as the theology of orders changes, so too will the law.

2. Throughout this essay, I will use *priesthood* to include both of the sacerdotal orders: bishops and presbyters. When referring simply to the second order of ordained ministry, I will use *presbyter*.

3. *Lumen gentium* (hereafter cited as *LG*) #29, in *Decrees of the Ecumenical Councils*, 2 vols., ed. Norman P. Tanner (Washington, DC: Georgetown University Press, 1990), 2:874; translation mine. I prefer to translate *in diaconia liturgiae, verbi et caritatis* as "in a service of liturgy, of the Word, and of charity" because the Council fathers applied the term *diaconia* to the full, triple *munus* of the bishop. Presbyters and deacons participate in lesser degrees in this apostolic *diaconia*. Some people tend to apply *diaconia* to the third element of the *munus*, giving the impression that "service" is simply part of it; actually, following the usage of the Council, the entire *munus* is *diaconia*.

4. Ibid.

5. This may be seen in recent statements from the Holy See, such as the multidicasterial "Instruction on Certain Questions Regarding the Collaboration of the Non-Ordained Faithful in the Sacred Ministry of the Priest" (Vatican City: Libreria Editrice Vaticana, 1997). Notice that even in the title, the laity are not referred to according to their baptismal status but rather according to what they are not.

6. James H. Provost, "Permanent Deacons in the 1983 Code," in *Canon Law Society of America Proceedings* 46 (1984): 175.

7. International Theological Commission, *Le Diaconat: Evolution et Perspectives, Note Preliminaire* (September 30, 2002).

8. Dicasteries contributing to the Instruction were the Congregation for the Clergy, Pontifical Council for the Laity, Congregation for the Doctrine of the Faith, Congregation for Divine Worship and the Discipline of the Sacraments, Congregation for Bishops, Congregation for the Evangelization of Peoples, Congregation for Institutes of Consecrated Life and Societies of Apostolic Life, and Pontifical Council for the Interpretation of Legislative Texts.

9. International Theological Commission, *From the Diakonia of Christ to the Diakonia of the Apostles: An Historico-Theological Research Document* (London: The Incorporated Catholic Truth Society, 2003).

10. *Catéchisme de l'Église Catholique* (Ottawa: Conférence des Évêques catholiques du Canada, 1993), #875: "De Lui, ils reçoivent la mission et la faculté (le « pouvoir sacré ») d'agir *in persona Christi Capitis*."

11. *Catechismus Catholicae Ecclesiae* (Vatican City: Libreria Editrice Vaticana, 1997), #875: "Ab Eo Episcopi et presbyteri missionem et facultatem ('sacram potestam') agendi *in persona Christi Capitis* accipiunt, diaconi vero vim

populo Dei serviendi in *diakonia* liturgiae, verbi et caritatis, in communione cum Episcopo eiusque presbyterio."

12. John Paul II, apostolic letter, *Ordinatio Sacerdotalis*, May 22, 1994, #4.

13. Congregation for the Doctrine of the Faith, "Concerning the Teaching Contained in Ordinatio Sacerdotalis Responsum ad Dubium," October 28, 1995.

14. Congregation for the Clergy et al., "Instruction on Certain Questions Regarding the Collaboration of the Non-Ordained Faithful in the Sacred Ministry of Priests" (Vatican City: Libreria Editrice Vaticana, 1997), ##29–35; in the last paragraph, the Instruction cites the *Catechism of the Catholic Church*, #876.

15. Phil 2:1–11.

16. Phil 2:2.

17. Phil 2:3–4.

18. Phil 2:5–11.

19. See William T. Ditewig, *The Emerging Diaconate: Servant Leaders in a Servant Church* (Mahwah, NJ: Paulist Press, 2007), especially chapter 5.

20. Consider, for example, Otto Pies, "Block 26: Erfahrungen aus dem Priesterleben in Dachau," *Stimmen der Zeit* 141 (1947–48): 10–28. Also Wilhelm Schamoni, *Familienväter als geweihte Diakone* (Paderborn: Schöningh, 1953); published in English as *Married Men as Ordained Deacons*, trans. Otto Eisner (London: Burns and Oates, 1955).

21. After writing several essays on the possibility of a renewed diaconate, Rahner devoted considerable time and attention on a substantive text that could be of use to the bishops gathering for the Council: Karl Rahner and Herbert Vorgrimler, eds., *Diakonia in Christo: Über die Erneuerung des Diakonates* (Freiburg: Herder, 1962).

22. Bishop León Bonaventura de Uriarte Bengoa, OFM (1891–1970) of San Ramon, Peru, asked that "deaconesses be instituted"; Bishop Giuseppe Ruotolo (1898–1970) of Ugento, Italy, suggested that "the order of deacons be restored and extended to women with the obligation of celibacy." *Acta et documenta Concilio oecumenico Vaticano II apparando; Series prima (antepraeparatoria)* (Typis Polyglottis Vaticanis, 1960–61) (*ADA*), II/II, 121.

23. *ADA*, II/II, 128–31.

24. Ibid.

25. Interesting is the lack of any mention of the ministry of deacons in charitable work.

26. *ADA*, II/II, 128–31.

27. During the conciliar debates themselves, the "mature age" for married deacons was reduced to thirty-five. The age for unmarried ordinands remained at twenty-five, and there was no mention of religious orders; the debates centered almost totally on secular clergy.

28. *Acta Synodalia Sacrasancti Concilii Vaticani II* (Typis Polyglottis Vaticanis, 1970) (*AS*), III/VIII, 53.

29. *AS*, II/II, 82–360.

30. *AS*, II/II, 227–30.

31. Some bishops felt that the question of the diaconate was simply a disciplinary issue, not appropriate for a dogmatic constitution. This view was in the minority, however, and the discussions and voting clearly desired that the diaconate be included in such a document.

32. *AS*, II/II, 229.

33. Ibid., II/II, 317–19.

34. Ibid., II/III, 199.

35. Pius XII, "Quelques aspects fondamentaux de l'apostolat des laïcs: Hiérarchie et Apostolat," *Acta Apostolicae Sedis* (*AAS*) 49 (1957): 925.

36. Leo Cardinal Suenens, "The Coresponsibility of Deacons," in *Diaconal Reader: Selected Articles from the Diaconal Quarterly*, ed. Rev. John J. Ziegler (Washington, DC: NCCB, 1985), 47.

37. Ibid.

38. *AS*, II/II, 319.

39. Cf. "Decree on the Catholic Eastern Churches" (Orientalium ecclesiarum), #17.

40. *Ad gentes*, #16.

41. Paul VI, *Hodie concilium*, *AAS* 58 (1966): 57–64.

42. John Paul II, "Allocution to the Permanent Deacons and Their Wives Given at Detroit, MI (September 19, 1987)," *Origins* 17 (1987): 327–29.

43. Benedict XVI, *Deus Caritas Est* (December 25, 2005), #21. Accessible at http://www.vatican.va/holy_father/benedict_xvi/encyclicals/documents/hf_ben-xvi_enc_20051225_deus-caritas-est_en.html.

44. International Theological Commission, *From the Diakonia of Christ to the Diakonia of the Apostles: An Historico-Theological Research Document* (London: Catholic Truth Society, 2003), 98. This is an unofficial translation of the original French.

45. Pope John Paul II, general audience, "Deacons Serve the Kingdom of God" (October 5, 1993), 6.

46. International Theological Commission, 100.

47. Canon Law Society of America, *The Canonical Implications of Ordaining Women to the Permanent Diaconate: Report of an Ad Hoc Committee of the Canon Law Society of America* (Washington, DC: CLSA, 1995).

48. Ibid., 26.

49. Ibid., 50.

50. Ibid. For the question of the deacon and governance, which would apply to women deacons as well, see

William T. Ditewig, "The Exercise of Governance by Deacons: A Theological and Canonical Study" (PhD dissertation, Catholic University of America, 2002).

51. *AS*, II/II, 229.

## WOMEN DEACONS: FUTURE

1. "The question of ordaining women to the diaconate is 'not settled,' [Kasper] added, but women are already doing what they would be able to do if they were ordained as deacons." Tracy Early, "Ecumenism Undergoing 'Radical Change' in 21st Century, Cardinal Says," *Catholic News Service*, March 17, 2005.

2. Bishop Walter Kasper, "The Deacon offers an ecclesiological view of the present day challenges in the Church and Society" (paper, International Diaconate Center Study Conference, Brixen, Italy, October 1997).

3. Tracy Early, "Ecumenism," *Catholic News Service*.

4. *Notificazione delle Congregazioni per la Dottrina della Fede, per il Culto Divino e la Disciplina dei Sacramenti, per il Clero 1. Da taluni Paesi sono pervenute ai nostri Dicasteri alcune segnalazioni di programmazione e di svolgimento di corsi, direttamente o indirettamente finalizzati all'ordinazione diaconale delle donne. Si vengono così a determinare aspettative carenti di salda fondatezza dottrinale e che possono generare, pertanto, disorientamento pastorale. 2. Poiché l'ordinamento ecclesiale non prevede la possibilità di una tale ordinazione, non è lecito porre in atto iniziative che, in qualche modo, mirino a preparare candidate all'Ordine diaconale. 3. L'autentica promozione della donna nella Chiesa, in conformità al costante Magistero ecclesiastico, con speciale riferimento a quello di Sua Santità Giovanni Paolo II, apre altre ampie prospettive di servizio e di collaborazione. 4. Le Congre-*

*gazioni sottoscritte - nell'ambito delle proprie competenze - si rivolgono, pertanto, ai singoli Ordinari affinché vogliano spiegare ai propri fedeli ed applicare diligentemente la suindicata direttiva. Questa Notificazione è stata approvata dal Santo Padre, il 14 settembre 2001. Dal Vaticano, 17 settembre 2001.*

This is the original text. The following English translation is by Phyllis Zagano and Carmela Leonforte: 1. Reports have been received from certain countries of the planning and conduct of courses directly or indirectly aimed at the ordination of women deacons, raising expectations that have no firm doctrinal foundations and that may thus cause confusion in pastoral work. 2. Since the church law does not allow for such, it is not lawful to put in place initiatives that, somehow, are intended to prepare [women] candidates for the Order of deacon. 3. The authentic promotion of woman in the Church, according to the constant Magisterium of the Church, with special reference to His Holiness John Paul II, opens other ample prospects for their service and collaboration. 4. Therefore the undersigned Congregations, as far as their competence is concerned, are addressing the individual Ordinaries, urging them to explain to their parishioners the above mentioned guideline, as well as to apply it diligently. This Notification was approved by the Holy Father on the 14th of September 2001. By the Vatican on the 17th of September 2001.

The signers were Cardinals Joseph Ratzinger (Doctrine of the Faith), Jorge Arturo Medina Estévez (Divine Worship and the Sacraments), and Dario Castrillón Hoyos (Clergy). German Cardinal Ratzinger is now Pope Benedict XVI. Chilean Cardinal Medina Estévez and Colombian Cardinal Castrillón Hoyos have since retired.

5. English translation by Phyllis Zagano from the original French, which follows: "*Pour ce qui est de l'ordination des*

*femmes au diaconat, il convient de noter que deux indications importantes émergent de ce qui a été exposé jusqu'ici: 1) les diaconesses dont il est fait mention dans la Tradition de l'Église ancienne—selon ce que suggèrent le rite d'institution et les fonctions exercées—ne sont pas purement et simplement assimilables aux diacres; 2) l'unité du sacrement de l'ordre, dans la claire distinction entre les ministères de l'évêque et des presbytres d'une part et le ministère diaconal d'autre part, est fortement souligné par la Tradition ecclésiale, surtout dans la doctrine du concile Vatican II et l'enseignement postconciliaire du Magistère. À la lumière de ces éléments mis en évidence par la présente recherche historico-théologique, il reviendra au ministère de discernement que le Seigneur a établi dans son Église de se prononcer avec autorité sur la question."* "Le Diaconat" *La documentation catholique* (19 Janvier 2003) 23:107. The Commission maintains the singular word *ordre* found in *Catéchisme de l'Église catholique.* English language Canon Law (cc. 1008–54) uses *orders* and the *Catechism of the Catholic Church* (ch. 3, art. 6) uses *holy orders.* The original ITC document is in French. It was first published as *"Le Diaconat: Évolution et perspectives," La documentation catholique* (19 Janvier 2003) 23: 58–107, and in Italian, *"Il Diaconato: Evoluzione e Prospettive," La Civiltà Cattolica* 2003, I:253–336. The Vatican Web site publishes it solely in French: http://www.vatican.va/roman_curia/congregations /cfaith/cti_documents/rc_con_cfaith_pro_05072004_dia conate_fr.html. See also Phyllis Zagano, "Catholic Women Deacons: Present Tense," *Worship* 77, no. 5 (September 2003): 386–408, for a discussion of this document.

 6. Pope Benedict VIII's 1018 letter to the bishop of Porto in Portugal confirms and grants that diocesan ordinary's privileges in perpetuity to ordain priests, deacons or deaconesses (*diaconissis*), and subdeacons: "Paris modo con-

cedimus et confirmamus vobis vestrisque successoribus in perpetuum omnem ordinationem episcopalem, tam de presbyteris quam diaconibus vel diaconissis, seu subdiaconibus." Gary Macy, *The Hidden History of Women's Ordination* (New York: Oxford University Press, 2008), 35, 172–73. See also Kevin Madigan and Carolyn Osiek, *Ordained Women in the Catholic Church: A Documentary History* (Baltimore: Johns Hopkins University Press, 2005), 147. A footnote in the Madigan and Osiek book states that the letter comes from *Patrologia Latina*, ed. J.-P. Migne et al. (Paris: Garnieri Fratres, 1844–91), 139.1921; and that it is also reproduced in *Monumenta de viduis diaconissis virginibusque tractantia*, ed. Josephine Mayer, Florilegium Patristicum 42 (Bonn: Peter Hanstein, 1938), 52. The footnote also states that Pope Leo IX later reconfirmed this concession (PL 143–602).

7. Roger Gryson, *The Ministry of Women in the Early Church* (Collegeville, MN: Liturgical Press, 1976) (Translation of *Le ministère des femmes dans L'Église ancienne. Recherches et synthèses*, Section d'historire 4. Gembloux: J. Duculot, 1972), 63–64.

8. The Congregation for the Doctrine of the Faith's "General Decree regarding the delict of the sacred ordination of a woman" (December 19, 2007) states in part: "Both the one who attempts to confer a sacred order on a woman, and the woman who attempts to receive a sacred order, incur an excommunication *latae sententiae* reserved to the Apostolic See." *AAS* 100 (2008): 403, published in *L'Osservatore Romano*, May 30, 2008. The decree's intent was later restated by the Congregation within a long list of grave delicts, or "crimes," published in July 2010 with the approval of Pope Benedict XVI, but not bearing his signature. There, it is put as: "The more grave delict of the attempted sacred ordination of a woman is also reserved to the Congregation for the

Doctrine of the Faith: 1° With due regard for can. 1378 of the Code of Canon Law, both the one who attempts to confer sacred ordination on a woman, and she who attempts to receive sacred ordination, incurs a *latae sententiae* excommunication reserved to the Apostolic See." http://www. usccb.org/mr/Norms-English.pdf (accessed September 10, 2010).

9. The letter of Epiphanius of Salamis to John of Jerusalem comes to mind. Epiphanius apologizes for ordaining one of John's men to the priesthood, pointing out, however, that the ordination took place in a monastery and was therefore beyond John's jurisdiction. Within the letter, Epiphanius says he never ordained a woman as deacon to serve in another bishop's diocese, clearly implying that John did so. Epiphanius wrote: "Numquam autem ego ordinavi diaconissas etam alienas misi provincias neque feci quidquam, ut ecclesiam scinderem." Josephine Mayer, *Monumenta de viduis diaconissis virginibusque tractantia. Florilegium patristicum tam veteris quam medii aevi auctores complectens*, 42 (Bonn: Peter Hanstein, 1938), 12.

10. *Acta et documenta Concilio oecuminco Vaticano II apparando; Series prima (antepraeparatoria)* (Typis Polyglottis Vaticanis, 1960–61) (*ADA*), II/II, 121.

11. *Il Regno* (July 19, 1985), as cited in Janine Hourcade, *Les diaconesses dans l'Eglise d'hier et de demain* (Saint-Maurice: Saint-Augustin, 2001), 21.

12. Martini called for *"l'ordinazione delle donne al diaconato, almeno"* at the European Bishops' Synod in 1999. Sandro Magister, *"Vade retro, Concilio," L'Espresso* (February 17, 2000). Others who were assumed to support the notion at the time were Timothy Radcliffe, OP, then master of the Order of Preachers; Cardinal Karl Lehmann, bishop of Mainz; John R. Quinn, retired archbishop of San Francisco; and

Cardinal Pierre Eyt, archbishop of Bordeaux, who died in 2001. Basil Cardinal Hume died a few months before this synod.

13. John L. Allen, Jr., "The Word from Rome," *National Catholic Reporter* 3:13 (November 21, 2003). http://www.nationalcatholicreporter.org/word/word112103.htm (accessed January 25, 2011).

14. See "Catholic Women's Ordination: The Ecumenical Implications of Women Deacons in the Armenian Apostolic Church, the Orthodox Church of Greece, and Union of Utrecht Old Catholic Churches," *Journal of Ecumenical Studies* 43, no. 1 (Winter 2008): 124–37. Editing errors in the print publication have been corrected, with the corrected article at http://www.nwcu.org/Documents/Zagano-JES-corrected 23APR10.pdf. See also Roberta R. Ervine, "The Armenian Church's Women Deacons," *St. Nersess' Theological Review* 12 (2007): 17–56.

15. "Bartholomew said that there were no canonical reasons why women could not be ordained deacons in the Orthodox Church." National Conference of Catholic Bishops, "News about the Eastern Churches and Ecumenism," No. 5 (February, 1996), 1, reporting from *Service Orthodoxe de Presse, "Geneve: visite du patriarche oecuméique en Suisse,"* No. 204 (janvier 1996), 3.

16. See Phyllis Zagano, "The Question of Governance and Ministry for Women," *Theological Studies* 68, no. 2 (June 2007): 348–67.

17. Cardinal Kasper was the messenger to the Church of England when its Lambeth Conference debated the notion of women as bishops in that mother church of the Anglican Communion, a notion that they eventually approved. See Kasper's address, "Mission of Bishops in the Mystery of the Church: Reflections on the question of ordaining women to

episcopal office in the Church of England," at http://www. vatican.va/roman_curia/pontifical_councils/chrstuni/card-kasper-docs/rc_pc_chrstuni_doc_20060605 _kasper-bishops _en.html (accessed May 17, 2010).

18. http://www.zenit.org/article-24084?l=english (accessed May 5, 2011).

19. Canon 861.2.

20. Canon 767 restricts the homily to *sacerdoti aut diacono*, that is, to bishops, priests, and deacons. An interpretation of canon 767:1 by the Pontifical Council on Interpretation of Legislative Texts (May 26, 1987) overrides the dispensary power of the diocesan ordinary of canon 87 and states that he cannot allow others to preach. There is deep ecclesiastical traction against preaching by laypersons. Typically, the presider is to preach: "The homily should ordinarily be given by the priest celebrant." The Sacred Congregation for Divine Worship, *General Instruction of the Roman Missal*, trans. ICEL (Washington, USCC, 1977), 42. Laypersons can preach at Masses for children according to the Sacred Congregation for Divine Worship, *Directory for Masses With Children* (November 1, 1972), 24. In 1997, eight dicasteries restated the prohibition against lay preaching: "The homily...must be reserved to the sacred minister, priest or deacon, to the exclusion of the non-ordained faithful, even if these should have responsibilities as 'pastoral assistants' or catechists in whatever type of community or group. This exclusion is not based on the preaching ability of sacred ministers nor their theological preparation, but on that function which is reserved to them in virtue of having received the Sacrament of Holy Orders." Congregation for the Clergy, "Some Questions Regarding Collaboration of Nonordained Faithful in Priests' Sacred Ministry" (August 15, 1997), 3.

21. The 1917 Code allowed only clerics to be judges, and the authority of the judge was seen to be a delegated authority. Developments in procedural law allowed qualified laymen (1971) and, later, laywomen (1983 Code) to serve as judges as part of a tribunal (canon 1421), but the authority of the diocesan judge now seems to be ordinary power. See Lawrence G. Wrenn, "Book VII Processes," in *New Commentary on the Code of Canon Law*, eds. J. P. Beal, J. A. Corriden, and T. J. Green (New York and Mahwah, NJ: Paulist Press, 2000), 1624. Since non-clerics can "cooperate with" but not "participate in" governance, the lay judge is restricted from sole acts of judgment. Note the beginning of canon 129: "1. Those who have received sacred orders are qualified, according to the norm of the prescripts of the law, for the power of governance, which exists in the Church by divine institution and is also called the power of jurisdiction. 2. Lay members of the Christian faithful can cooperate in the exercise of this same power according to the norm of law." Benedict XVI wrote the revised canon 129. See Elizabeth McDonough, "Jurisdiction Exercised by Non-Ordained Members in Religious Institutes," *Canon Law Society of America Proceedings* 58 (1996): 292–307. McDonough refers to Cardinal Ratzinger's animadversiones and suggested text of December 22, 1980, in Congregation Plenaria, 294, fn.4.

22. See, for example, Manfred Hauke, *Die Problematik um das Frauenpriestertum vor dem Hintergrund der Schöpfungs- und Erlösungsordnung* (Paderborn: Verlag Bonifatius-Druckerei, 1988), translated by David Kipp as *Women in the Priesthood? A Systematic Analysis in the Light of the Order of Creation and Redemption* (San Francisco: Ignatius Press, 1988); Gerhard Müller, *Priestertum und Diakonat: Der Empfänger des Weihesakramentes in schöpfungstheologischer und christologischer Perspektive* (Freiburg:

Johannes Verlag, 2000), translated by Michael J. Miller as *Priesthood and Diaconate: The Recipient of the Sacrament of Holy Orders from the Perspective of Creation Theology and Christology* (San Francisco: Ignatius Press, 2002); Sara Butler, *The Catholic Priesthood and Women: A Guide to the Teaching of the Church* (Chicago: Hillenbrand Books, 2007).

23. For example, Balsamon's commentary on canon 15 of the Council of Chalcedon notes that women may not enter the sanctuary, and his "Response to Mark's Question 35" says women are barred from the sacred because of the "monthly affliction." Madigan and Osiek, *Ordained Women*, 136.

24. Relatively recent scholarship reacts negatively to the relationship between the post-Reformation Carthusian ritual and earlier, now lost, Carthusian rituals, which might demonstrate closer connections to diaconal ordination. See Daniel Le Blévec, « La Consecration des Moniales Cartusiennes d'apres un Pontifical Romain conserve a Avignon (Bibl. mun. 205), » in J. Hogg, A. Girard, and D. Le Blévec, *Analecta Cartusiana 208, Études et Documents pour L'Histoire des Chartreux* (Salzburg, Austria: Institut Für Anglistik und Amerikanistik Universität Salzburg, 2003), 203–19. Aimé George Martimort, in *Deaconesses: An Historical Study* (San Francisco: Ignatius Press, 1986) (a translation of *Les Diaconesses: Essai Historique*. Rome: Edizioni Liturgiche, 1982), 235–40, notes that others find differently: Y. Gourdel, Chartreux, in *Dictionnaire de spiritualitié*....vol. 2 (1953), col. 721; M. de Fontette, *Recherches sur les origins de moniales chartreuses*, in *Etudes d'historie et de droit canoniques dediées à Gabriel Le Bras*, vol. 2 (Paris: Sirey, 1963), 1150–51; L. Ray and P. Mouton, *Chartreuses (Règle des moniales)*, in *Dictionnaire de droit canoniques*, vol. 3 (1942), cols. 630–32. Also in support of the connection is Nathalie Nabert, *Les moniales chartreuses* (Geneva: Ad Solem 2009), 53–61.

25. In addition to writing the opening section of this book, Gary Macy has expertly reviewed the history of the ordination of women deacons in "What Does the Ordination of Women Then Mean for Women Now?" *Journal of Religion & Society* (Supplement Series 5, 2009): 137–47.

26. Jean Daniélou, *The Ministry of Women in the Church*, trans. Glyn Simon (London: Faith Press, Ltd., 1974), 29; also, "Le Ministerè des femmes dans l'Église ancienne," *La Maison Dieu* 61 (1960), 94. Daniélou interprets Epiphanius's words to mean that women deacons annointed women.

27. Congregation for the Doctrine of the Faith, "Note on the Minister of the Sacrament of the Anointing of the Sick" (February 11. 2005). http://www.vatican.va/roman_curia/congregations/cfaith/documents/rc_con_cfaith_doc_20050 211_unzione-infermi_en.html (accessed June 15, 2010).

28. Clerics who belong to religious institutes or orders are incardinated into those religious institutes and orders, which have few permanent deacons, and to the personal prelature of Opus Dei, which has none.

29. One example is the Abbey of Santa Maria la Real de Las Huelgas, whose abbess held this authority in perpetuity until it was canceled by Pius IX.

30. Regarding the "quasi-episcopal" authority of an abbess: a Cistercian abbess, for example, has a ring, a pectoral cross, and a crosier as symbols of her office.

31. Ordination of a lay monastic elected as abbot is not unheard of. When the Benedictine monks of Glenstal Abbey, Co. Limerick, Ireland, elected Br. Mark Patrick Hederman fifth abbot in 2008, he was subsequently ordained deacon and priest before his abbatial consecration.

32. Canon 1192, par. 2.

33. CICLSAL directed the 2009 to 2011 apostolic visitation of U.S.–based apostolic women religious, both diocesan

and papal. Contemplative houses of nuns were exempt. Nearly concurrently, the Congregation for the Doctrine of the Faith conducted an investigation of the Leadership Conference of Women Religious, the main membership organization for heads of women's apostolic institutes.

34. It is not at all clear that any women's institutes would choose to become mixed clerical and lay. By way of contrast, in 2002, the Congregation of Christian Brothers general chapter considered and dismissed a proposal that its members be ordained. They were founded in Ireland in 1802 to provide Catholic education to the materially poor.

35. For a fuller discussion of the question of mixed clerical and lay institutes, see Phyllis Zagano, "Women Religious, Women Deacons?" *Review for Religious* 60, no. 3 (May–June 2001): 230–44.

36. National Conference of Catholic Bishops, Bishops' Committee on the Permanent Diaconate, *Permanent Deacons in the United States: Guidelines on Their Formation and Ministry*, rev. ed. (Washington, DC: National Conference of Catholic Bishops, 1971, 1985). United States Conference of Catholic Bishops, Bishops' Committee on the Permanent Diaconate, *National Directory for the Formation, Ministry and Life of Permanent Deacons in the United States* (Washington, DC: United States Conference of Catholic Bishops, 2005).

37. One early study is Rebecca Meehan, "The Deacon's Wife: An Emerging Role," in *The Deacon Reader*, ed. James Keating (New York and Mahwah, NJ: Paulist Press, 2006), 232–47. This is not to suggest that merely completing the training program certifies a vocation to the diaconate, for either husband or wife.

38. The age requirement of thirty-five for both married and unmarried deacons is particular law in the United States.

The universal law requires an ordinand to be twenty-five, thirty-five if married.

39. The situation of a young woman ordained to the diaconate would be similar to that of a consecrated virgin. While the secular woman who makes a consecration of virginity is under the care of her bishop, she is owed no support from him and is expected to find her own way in life. There are fewer than 150 consecrated virgins in the United States, but their modest numbers are increasing. The rite for consecration of virginity was restored in 1970.

40. A law of Theodosius from 390 set the minimum age of women deacons at sixty. The Council of Chalcedon of 451 set the minimum age at forty. Aimé Georges Martimort, *Deaconesses: An Historical Study* (San Francisco: Ignatius Press, 1986), 107–9.